MISCELLANEOUS ARCHAEOLOGICAL STUDIES IN THE
ANAMAX-ROSEMONT LAND EXCHANGE AREA

by

Martyn D. Tagg
Richard G. Ervin
Bruce B. Huckell

Submitted by

Cultural Resource Management Division
Arizona State Museum
University of Arizona

Prepared for

ANAMAX Mining Company

1984

Archaeological Series No. 147, Vol. 4

CONTENTS

FIGURES   vi

TABLES   viii

PREFACE   x

ACKNOWLEDGMENTS   xii

ABSTRACT   xiii

Chapter
1   LITHIC MATERIAL PROCUREMENT SITES IN THE ROSEMONT AREA
     Richard G. Ervin and Martyn D. Tagg   1
     Environment   2
     Site Descriptions   2
         AZ EE:2:90   4
             Area A   5
             Area B   7
         AZ EE:2:131   9
         AZ EE:2:135   12
         X85-S1-L1 and X85-S3-L1   14
         AZ EE:2:91   15
         AZ EE:2:89   15
         Summary   17
     Analysis   17
         Research Objectives   21
         Definitions and Assumptions   21
         Samples   23
         Analytical Methods   23
             Raw Material   25
                 Silicified Limestone   25
                 Quartzite   25
                 Metasediment   27
                 Other Materials   27
             Artifact Type   27
                 Complete Flake   27
                 Split Flake   27
                 Proximal Flake Fragment   27
                 Distal and Medial Flake Fragment   28
                 Shatter   28
                 Retouched Piece   28
                 Core   28
                 Core-Hammerstone   28
             Platform Type   28
                 Cortical   29
                 Plain   29

Faceted   29
Indeterminate   29
Unidirectional   29
Bidirectional   29
Multidirectional   29
Cortex   30
Lipping   30
Patination   30
Other Attributes   31
Flake Dimensions   31
Retouched Pieces   32
Artifact Size   32
Retouch Type   32
Retouched Piece Type   32
Scrapers   33
Denticulates   33
Irregularly Retouched Pieces   33
Miscellaneous Unifacially Retouched Pieces   33
Bifacially Retouched Pieces   33
Projectile Points   34
Choppers   34
Wear Patterns   34
Patina   34
Data Presentation and Comparisons   34
Raw Material   35
Artifact Type   35
Platform Type   35
Cortex   41
Lipping   41
Patination   41
Flake Dimensions   41
Retouched Pieces   50
Wear Patterns on Retouched Pieces   54
Interpretations   54
Conclusions   57

2   THE SYCAMORE CANYON SITES
Martyn D. Tagg and Bruce B. Huckell   61
Environment   61
Site Descriptions   65
AZ EE:2:100   65
Features   67
Feature 1   67
Feature 2   67
Feature 3   67
AZ EE:2:101   69
Features   69
Feature 1   71
Feature 2   71
Feature 3   71

Analysis of Artifacts   71
    Flaked Stone   73
        Debitage   74
            Methods of Study   74
            Results   74
        Retouched Pieces   76
            Methods of Study   82
            Results   85
        Discussion   92
    Ceramics   93
        Plain Ware   93
        Decorated Ware   94
        Red Ware   96
        Worked Sherds   96
        Discussion   96
    Ground Stone   98
        Manos   99
        Metates   99
        Pitted Stone   100
        Miscellaneous Ground Stone   101
        Discussion   101
    Bone   101
Interpretations   102
    AZ EE:2:100   103
        Archaic Period   103
        Ceramic Period   103
        Protohistoric-Historic Period   104
    AZ EE:2:101   104
Conclusions   105

3   SOBAIPURI SITES IN THE ROSEMONT AREA
    Bruce B. Huckell   107
    AZ EE:2:80   109
        Features   111
        Artifact Assemblage   113
        Summary   114
    AZ EE:2:95   114
        Features   116
        Artifact Assemblage   117
            Ceramics   117
            Flaked Stone   117
            Ground Stone   118
            European Trade Item   119
        Summary   119
    AZ EE:2:83   119
        Features   120
        Artifact Assemblage   123
            Ceramics   125
            Flaked Stone   125
            Ground Stone   127
            European Trade Items   127
        Summary   128
    Discussion   129

4   RESIDENTIAL TERRACES AT AZ EE:2:191
        A LATE RINCON/EARLY TANQUE VERDE SITE IN THE SANTA RITAS
        Martyn D. Tagg   131
        Environment   131
        Site Description   133
            Feature 1   133
            Feature 2   136
        Artifact Assemblage   136
            Ceramics   136
                Plain Ware   136
                Decorated Ceramics   140
            Flaked Stone   141
            Ground Stone   141
        Pollen and Flotation Analyses   143
        Discussion   143
        Conclusions   146

REFERENCES   147

FIGURES

1.1   Map of Rosemont area showing quarry site locations.   3

1.2   Map of AZ EE:2:90, Area A.   6

1.3   Map of AZ EE:2:90, Area B.   8

1.4   Map of AZ EE:2:131.   10

1.5   Map of AZ EE:2:135.   13

1.6   Map of AZ EE:2:91.   16

1.7   Map of AZ EE:2:89.   18

1.8   Two different types of quarry sites in the Rosemont area.   20

1.9   Artifact type frequencies.   38

1.10   Cortex frequencies for flakes.   45

1.11   Flake length frequencies for all samples.   46

1.12   Flake width frequencies for all samples.   47

1.13   Flake thickness frequencies for all samples.   48

1.14   Maximum size frequencies for broken flakes.   49

1.15   Retouched pieces from AZ EE:2:131.   52

1.16   Retouched pieces from AZ EE:2:135.   53

2.1   Location of the Sycamore Canyon parcel.   62

2.2   Locations of AZ EE:2:100 and AZ EE:2:101 in Sycamore Canyon.   64

2.3   Map of AZ EE:2:100.   66

2.4   Feature 1 at AZ EE:2:100.   68

2.5   Feature 2 at AZ EE:2:100.   68

2.6   Feature 3 before excavation at AZ EE:2:100.   68

2.7   Feature 3 after excavation at AZ EE:2:100.   68

2.8   Map of AZ EE:2:101.   70

2.9   Feature 1 at AZ EE:2:101.   72

2.10   Feature 2 at AZ EE:2:101.   72

2.11   Feature 3 at AZ EE:2:101 before excavation.   72

2.12   Feature 3 at AZ EE:2:101 after excavation.   72

2.13   Debitage size classes.   75

2.14   Frequencies of flaked stone debitage classes for the
        Sycamore Canyon sites, Rosemont Archaic sites, and
        Rosemont Hohokam sites.   77

2.15   Debitage size distribution for the Sycamore Canyon sites,
        Rosemont Archaic sites, and Rosemont Hohokam sites.   78

2.16   Raw material types for debitage from the Sycamore Canyon
        sites, Rosemont Archaic sites, and Rosemont Hohokam sites.   79

2.17   Relative quantities of cortex on debitage from the Sycamore
        Canyon sites, Rosemont Archaic sites, and Rosemont Hohokam
        sites.   80

2.18   Types of striking platforms on debitage from the Sycamore
        Canyon sites, Rosemont Archaic sites, and Rosemont Hohokam
        sites.   81

2.19   Frequencies of retouched tools from the Sycamore Canyon
        sites, Rosemont Archaic sites, and Rosemont Hohokam sites.   86

2.20   Projectile points from the Sycamore Canyon sites.   88

3.1   Location of Sobaipuri sites in the Rosemont area.   108

3.2   Map of AZ EE:2:80.   110

3.3   Map of Feature 4 at AZ EE:2:80.   112

3.4   Map of AZ EE:2:95.   115

3.5   Artifacts from AZ EE:2:95.   118

3.6   Map of AZ EE:2:83.   121

3.7   Map of Feature 1 at AZ EE:2:83.   122

3.8   Map of Feature 7 at AZ EE:2:83.   124

3.9   Artifacts from AZ EE:2:83.   128

4.1   General location of AZ EE:1:91 within the exchange area.   132

4.2   Map of AZ EE:1:91.   134

4.3   Map of Feature 1, AZ EE:1:91.   135

4.4   Reworked partial vessels from AZ EE:1:91.   139

4.5   Trincheras and agricultural sites with dry-laid rock
        features in and near the Tucson Basin.   144

TABLES

1.1   Lithic artifact attributes   24

1.2   Observations made on retouched pieces   26

1.3   Material type frequencies   36

1.4   Artifact type frequencies   37

1.5   Platform type frequencies for flakes   39

1.6   Platform type frequencies for cores   40

1.7   Cortex frequencies for flakes   42

1.8   Cortex frequencies for flake fragments   43

1.9   Cortex frequencies for cores   44

1.10   Retouched pieces from the lithic material procurement
        sites   51

2.1   Classes of artifacts and bone from the Sycamore Canyon
        sites   73

2.2   Flaked stone debitage and cores from the Sycamore Canyon
        sites   76

2.3   Tabulation of retouched pieces and cores from the Sycamore
      Canyon sites   83

2.4   Tabulation of ceramics by unit and level at AZ EE:2:100   97

2.5   Tabulation of ground stone artifacts at AZ EE:2:100   98

3.1   Attributes of Feature 4 at AZ EE:2:80   111

3.2   Attributes of Feature 1 at AZ EE:2:95   116

3.3   Attributes of structures at AZ EE:2:83   123

3.4   Flaked stone artifacts from AZ EE:2:83   126

4.1   Distribution of artifacts at AZ EE:1:91   137

4.2   Distribution of ceramics by feature at AZ EE:1:91   138

4.3   Flaked stone artifacts from AZ E:1:91   142

PREFACE

Bruce B. Huckell

This, the final volume of the ANAMAX-Rosemont Project report series, is a collection of four short studies that were conducted as part of our effort to document and understand the human occupation of the northern Santa Rita Mountains. In contrast to the preceding three volumes, these studies do not form a single temporally or culturally definable unit, but rather are quite divergent in subject matter from previous volumes and from one another. While each has something to contribute to the story of human occupation in the land exchange area, none could be easily accomodated in the three previous volumes due to one or more geographic or occupational factors that will be discussed in the following paragraphs.

Chapter 1 reports the results of investigations at three lithic material quarry sites located on the east side of the ridgeline of the Santa Rita Mountains in the Rosemont area. These three sites represent what had been, prior to the re-drawing of the eastern boundary of the exchange area, a rather extensive class of sites. The movement of the eastern boundary further to the west resulted in the elimination of several of these sites, including some of the larger and more intensively used ones. This forced us to lessen the level of effort pursued at this class of sites, but nevertheless the study conducted by Richard Ervin and Martyn Tagg serves as an excellent characterization of the prehistoric use of the lithic raw material available in the Rosemont area. Because of a lack of culturally or temporally diagnostic artifacts at most of these sites and evidence that they saw sporadic use over long periods of time, it was not possible to integrate this study with either the Archaic or Hohokam volumes. It is presented here as an example of the use of a particular critical resource over several millenia by most, if not all, of the prehistoric groups who called this area theirs.

In late 1980 and early 1981 ANAMAX requested the addition of three new parcels to the proposed land exchange. Two of these parcels, in their entirety, and a portion of the third parcel are located completely outside the Barrel Canyon drainage net which at the close of the testing phase had been singled out as a naturally bounded area that could serve as the basis for organizing the mitigation phase research. The survey of the largest of the three parcels, Sycamore Canyon, revealed the presence of two prehistoric sites apparently of Archaic age with minor Ceramic period components. The mitigation phase work for the Archaic period sites was modified to include these two sites, but excavations at both quickly revealed that they were in fact rather thoroughly mixed Archaic, Hohokam, and Protohistoric/Early Historic occupations. Due to this admixture, as well as their location in a different environmental setting on the west side of the ridgeline, these sites were not included in either the Archaic or Hohokam studies. Chapter 2 presents the results of our excavations at AZ EE:2:100 and AZ EE:2:101 in Sycamore Canyon, and serves to document the reuse of the same site area for short periods of time over several thousand years. While much dryer and less heavily forested than the Rosemont area to the southeast, Sycamore Canyon nevertheless afforded plant and animal resources in sufficient quantities to be attractive to a variety of cultural groups over a long period.

Also eliminated from further work by the rearrangement of the eastern boundary of the exchange area were three small Sobaipuri or Upper Pima sites. All three were examined on a limited scale during the 1979 testing phase and, in view of the results obtained, it was decided to make this material available in published form. Chapter 3 is devoted to the description of these loci, and is a slightly modified version of a chapter included in the unpublished testing phase report (Huckell 1980). It is hoped that the results of this limited work will help to expand our understanding of the final native occupants of the Rosemont area and southeastern Arizona.

The fourth and final chapter by Martyn Tagg presents the results of limited excavations undertaken at AZ EE:1:91, a small Hohokam site located on the west side of the ridgeline of the Santa Rita Mountains. Lying a short distance east and south of the historic townsite of Hevetia, this site was located in late 1980 during a survey of a parcel newly added to the exchange area. The site was mapped and test excavated at the end of the field work on the Rosemont Hohokam sites, but was not presented with them due to its geographic separation from those along Barrel Canyon. It is in several respects an unusual site, particularly in that it contains several rock terraces or trincheras that apparently served as residential localities.

While all of these reports are quite short, they serve to further emphasize the range of prehistoric and early historic use of one small part of the mountains of southeastern Arizona.

ACKNOWLEDGMENTS

Thanks are due a number of individuals for their aid and assistance in producing this volume. First our gratitude goes to ANAMAX Mining Company for their generous support of the work in the Rosemont area; their patience and understanding throughout the project have been most appreciated. In particular, the efforts of John Frankovich, Will McCurry, and Burt Reed are acknowledged.

The investigation of these sites involved work by a number of different people at different times throughout the course of the project. Thanks are first extended to Cynthia Graff and Susan Wells, for they worked with Rick Ervin and Marty Tagg through a cold, windy November and December to excavate the lithic material procurement sites reported in Chapter 1. Sue, Cynthia, Rick, and Marty were also crew members during the investigation of the Sycamore Canyon sites (Chapter 2) along with Ron Beckwith, Teri Cleeland, Banks Leonard, and Marilyn Saul. Ken Rozen served ably as assistant field supervisor during that portion of the work. The 1979 work at the Sobaipuri sites (Chapter 3) involved Earl Sires (assistant field supervisor), Peter Donelan, Jonathan Rossen, and Wayne Rottman, while work at AZ EE:1:91 (Chapter 4) in 1982 was accomplished by Alan Ferg (field supervisor), Allan Bannister, James Bayman, Wayne Ferguson, and Doak McDuffie. Charles Sternberg also contributed his time to map AZ EE:1:91 and AZ EE:2:90, one of the lithic material procurement sites.

Arthur Vokes and several student laboratory assistants processed all of the artifacts from the sites, and organized the materials for analysis. Ken Rozen and Bill Deaver aided greatly in helping to make sense of the flaked stone artifacts and the pottery, respectively, from the lithic material procurement sites, the Sycamore Canyon sites, and AZ EE:1:91.

Several people helped in the production of this report volume. Editorial expertise was provided by Barbara Crowl, and the final manuscript was typed by Michaline Cardella, Cathy Carver, and Robin Dyson. The artifact photographs in Chapters 1, 2, and 4 are the work of Janelle Weakley. Helga Teiwes produced the photograph used in Figure 3.5, and Ron Beckwith drew the artifacts shown in Figure 3.9. Charles Sternberg used his drafting talents to produce all of the site and feature maps, as well as the graphs in Chapters 1 and 2. Brian Byrd drew the map reproduced as Figure 2.2. Finally, Lynn Teague, Head of the Cultural Resource Management Division and Co-Principal Investigator on the ANAMAX-Rosemont Project, is thanked for her aid and support.

ABSTRACT

The four studies contained in this volume report the results of work undertaken at a number of different types of sites in the northern Santa Rita Mountains of southeastern Arizona. All these studies were performed within the ANAMAX-Rosemont land exchange area in the Coronado National Forest as part of a 10-month-long mitigation effort conducted by the Arizona State Museum.

Chapter 1 presents a description of detailed investigations at lithic material procurement sites in the Rosemont area. Two types of lithic material procurement sites are identified and described, and the kinds of flaked stone artifacts present at these sites are analyzed and discussed in detail. Evidence suggests that the majority of these sites resulted from the rather casual, nonintensive reduction of cobbles of quartzite and metasediment or, in one case, a relatively intensive utilization of two bedrock outcrops of silicified limestone. While most of the artifacts present at these sites are debitage, cores, and tested pieces, a few finished, retouched artifacts at certain of these sites suggest the possibility that activities other than the reduction of lithic raw materials were also pursued on a limited basis.

Chapter 2 describes the investigation of two sites in Sycamore Canyon, which is a major drainage system on the west side of the ridgeline of the Santa Rita Mountains, 5 km northwest of Rosemont. Excavation of the two sites produced relatively abundant quantities of artifacts representing occupations ranging from the Middle Archaic period through the Historic period. Detailed comparisons of the flaked stone asemblages from the Sycamore Canyon sites are made with those from the Archaic and Hohokam sites in the Rosemont area, and allow the inference that most of the occupation at the Sycamore Canyon sites occurred during the Archaic period. It is further suggested that both sites were used as temporary campsites for the seasonal exploitation of wild plant and animal resources during prehistoric and early historic times.

The third chapter presents data from test excavations carried out at three Sobaipuri of Upper Piman sites located in the Rosemont area. These sites were investigated in 1979, but adjustments to the land exchange boundaries resulted in their ultimate exclusion from the exchange area. The testing serves to document the presence of Sobaipuri residential sites in a montane setting, and indicates that at least two of the three were occupied shortly after Spanish contact.

Chapter 4 describes the investigation of a single site located at the western edge of the land exchange area near Helvetia. This site consists of residential structures positioned on artificially constructed rock terraces emplaced on steeply sloping topography. The recovered artifact assemblage suggests a late Rincon or early Tanque Verde phase age for the site. The limited nature of the work done at the site, coupled with an impoverished artifact assemblage, suggests that the site saw use for a short time, possibly seasonally, for an unknown purpose.

Chapter 1

LITHIC MATERIAL PROCUREMENT SITES
IN THE ROSEMONT AREA

Richard G. Ervin
Martyn D. Tagg

This report presents the results of investigations at three
lithic material procurement sites as part of the mitigation phase of the
ANAMAX-Rosemont Project. Also included is information on four
additional localities investigated in 1979 during the testing phase of
the project. In this report, a description of the sites and the
artifacts recovered from them is presented first. In addition, the
results of a formal analysis of the lithic debitage and retouched pieces
are presented. These data are used to help interpret the activities
which occurred at the sites and to gain some insight into the nature of
lithic material procurement in the Rosemont area.

Lithic material procurement sites were defined as sites that
lacked temporally diagnostic, finished flaked stone tools, but contained
abundant debitage, characteristics which suggested the procurement and
processing of lithic material (Huckell 1980: 4). Fifty-two such sites
are located in the area due to the abundance of quartzite, metasediment,
chert, and silicified limestone boulder gravels which compose the
sediments exposed on ridges throughout the Rosemont area. The
utilization of these exposed gravels is seen on most ridges, ranging
from a few flakes and cores to areas of dense lithic reduction (Huckell
1980: 198). From these sites, two large, and three small, quarry sites
were nonrandomly selected for the 1979 testing phase, with the major
goal of placing these sites within some sort of cultural and temporal
framework, and determining what elements of the stone tool assemblage
could be used in such an effort (Huckell 1980: 4). The results of the
testing indicated that this class of sites had the potential to yield
additional information of value, and it was recommended that a
10 percent sample of these sites be evaluated as part of the mitigation
phase (Huckell 1980: 270). Therefore, additional investigations of the
lithic material procurement sites were undertaken in December of 1982.
Of the 52 lithic material procurement sites identified prior to the
testing program, 8 had been eliminated in 1981 by revision of the
boundaries of the land exchange area. Of the remaining sites, a large
number were eliminated when the survey records were rechecked and the
sites were revisited. These were extremely low-density scatters of

1

unmodified flakes, and were judged to contain little significant information beyond that obtained during the survey. Even some of the sites that looked promising, based on the survey forms, turned out to be too impoverished in artifact density and diversity to yield additional significant information. Only two sites besides those visited during the testing program (AZ EE:2:131 and AZ EE:2:135) were found to warrant further investigation. In addition, further excavations were carried out at one site (AZ EE:2:90) that had been investigated during the testing program. Fieldwork began on December 7 and ran through December 20, 1982, and involved a crew of four archaeologists.

Environment

The Rosemont Study Area is located in the northern part of the Santa Rita Mountains, approximately 32 miles (51 km) southeast of Tucson, Arizona. On either side of the northwest trending ridgeline of the Santa Ritas are a series of bajadas and pediments which have been heavily dissected by headcutting drainages. These drainages have been incised 10 m to 30 m into the Tertiary and Quaternary gravels of which the piedmonts are composed. The present landscape, therefore, consists of numerous narrow, steep, flat-topped ridges separated by deeply incised valleys. Most of the prehistoric sites which have been located in the study area are situated on the flat ridgetops.

The study area is located primarily on the east side of the ridgeline of the Santa Rita Mountains, and all of the quarry sites are located along the Barrel Canyon drainage system (Fig. 1.1). Within this area Barrel Canyon has three major tributaries--McCleary Canyon, Wasp Canyon, and South Canyon--and is itself a tributary to Davidson Canyon, which drains into the Pantano Wash. Elevation in the study area ranges from 3800 feet to 6000 feet above sea level (Huckell 1980). In the past, the vegetation in the foothills of the Santa Ritas was primarily oak woodland and desert grassland, but since the introduction of cattle, one-seed juniper and mesquite have invaded the area at the expense of the oaks. Xeric hillslopes too dry to support trees are characterized by desert grassland communities, while oak-juniper woodlands occur on north-facing slopes at higher elevations. In addition, the canyon bottoms support a rich riparian community of oak, hackberry, walnut, desert willow, and mesquite trees.

Site Descriptions

This section contains descriptions of the specific environmental settings and artifact assemblages of seven lithic quarry sites, as well as brief descriptions of the investigations carried out at each site. The seven quarry sites include four investigated during the testing phase of the project (X85-S1-L1, X85-S3-S1, AZ EE:2:89, and AZ EE:2:91), two investigated during the mitigation phase (AZ EE:2:131 and

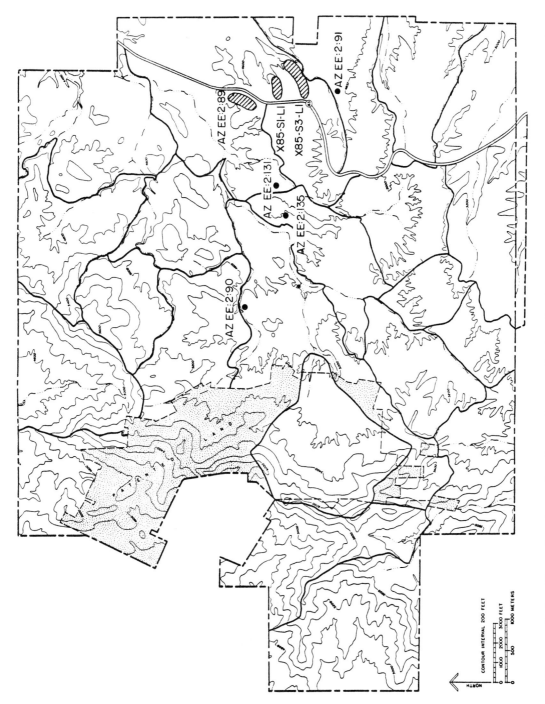

Figure 1.1   Map showing the locations of the lithic raw material procurement sites investigated during the testing and mitigation phases of the project.

AZ EE:2:135), and one that saw work during both the testing and mitigation phases (AZ EE:2:90).

AZ EE:2:90

AZ EE:2:90 is the most extensive lithic quarry site in the Rosemont area. Thousands of flakes littering the surface of the site attest to the extent of its use by the inhabitants of the area. Two separate silicified limestone bedrock outcrops, each consisting of a vertically tilted limestone bed, are located about 100 m apart along the crest of an east-west trending hill which forms the south bank of McCleary Canyon (Fig. 1.1). Each of the two outcrops is surrounded by a high density scatter of flakes, and were treated as separate areas during the 1979 testing phase and the 1982 mitigation phase of the project for two reasons. First, the two areas are spatially separate, with no artifacts occurring in the shallow saddle located between the outcrops. Second, the lithologic characteristics of the raw material from the two areas differ somewhat, raising the possibility that one or the other of the two loci might have been preferred for a given purpose at a certain point in time. The two loci of the site were given the designations Area A and Area B. It was decided to conduct additional investigations because of the high density of the artifact scatters at the site and the fact that large quantities of stone were being quarried from a bedrock source, making this site unique in the Rosemont area.

Since AZ EE:2:90 had been studied during the testing project, accurate contour maps were already available for each of the two separate areas that make up the site. After reestablishing the grid system, a number of 1-m-by-1-m squares were excavated in each area. These were judgmentally placed so as to provide excavated samples from both the dense, central part of the artifact scatter of each area and from the lower density surrounding scatter. Units were excavated in arbitrary 10 cm levels until sterile subsoil was reached, and all fill was screened through one-quarter inch mesh. In addition, retouched pieces and hammerstones observed on the general site surface were collected.

The vegetation at the site displays elements of both the desert grassland and oak woodland communities, and is dominated by grasses and mesquitilla. Juniper, oak and mesquite trees, as well as yucca and bear grass, are found on the site and on the north-facing hill slopes. To the north, McCleary Canyon supports a riparian community composed of oak, walnut, hackberry, and alligator bark juniper trees. Recent human disturbance on the site is minimal, consisting of a mining test pit and some isolated cartridge casings.

A fine- to medium-grained silicified limestone which "fractures predictably enough to be useful for a variety of purposes" outcrops at the two areas of the site (Huckell 1980: 207). The quality of the material is lessened by extensive natural fracture planes. Furthermore, between these fracture planes the material is characterized by occasional inclusions or flaws, which sometimes give flake surfaces an irregular appearance.

The length of time over which the limestone quarry has been used is not known. However, the wide range of patination which is present on the artifacts suggests a long period of exploitation. Although patination rates might have been influenced by several factors that could not be controlled during the artifact analysis, the marked differences that were observed strengthen the belief that the quarry was being utilized over a long period of time. This topic will be discussed in more detail in a later section.

In addition to the dense scatter of flakes on the surface of the site, other artifacts that were observed included a number of exhausted cores and tested pieces, as well as many unworked pieces apparently deemed unsuitable for knapping by the prehistoric artisans. By contrast, hammerstones were not evident in large numbers, although a few pieces of limestone exhibited the kind of battering typically produced during use as a hammerstone.

A number of retouched pieces exhibiting both unifacial and bifacial retouch were also visible on the surface. A total of 43 retouched pieces were recovered from AZ EE:2:90, 19 from the excavated grid squares, and an additional 24 that were observed on the surface and collected. The assemblage includes a large number of lightly or irregularly retouched pieces, in addition to more extensively retouched pieces similar to scrapers and denticulates. Most of the retouched pieces at AZ EE:2:90 probably represent attempts by flintknappers to assess the flaking qualities of a particular piece, based on the irregularity of the retouch and the lack of use-wear on the retouched edges.

Area A

Area A is located on a small, flat crest on the east end of the hilltop (Fig. 1.2). The material from Area A is dark gray in color and patinates to a bluish-gray or grayish-white color with increasing exposure and/or age (Huckell 1980: 209). This material is badly fractured, although to a somewhat lesser degree than the material which outcrops at Area B. The artifact scatter encompasses an area of about 900 square meters, but within this is a dense concentration of flaking debris of about 275 square meters surrounding the actual outcrop (Fig. 1.2). The surface artifact density ranges from 90 artifacts per square meter in the densest concentration to approximately 19 artifacts per square meter in the lighter surrounding scatter. The average density at the site is approximately 54 artifacts per square meter.

Two 1-m-by-1-m test squares were excavated within the densest concentration at Area A as part of the 1979 testing program. Upon returning to AZ EE:2:90 during the mitigation phase, these 1 m squares were expanded into 2-m-by-2-m units, and the remaining three-quarters of each was excavated. An additional 1 m square unit was excavated in the dense concentration, and three more 1 m squares were placed in the lighter surrounding scatter. This gives a total of twelve 1-m-by-1-m test units that were excavated at AZ EE:2:90.

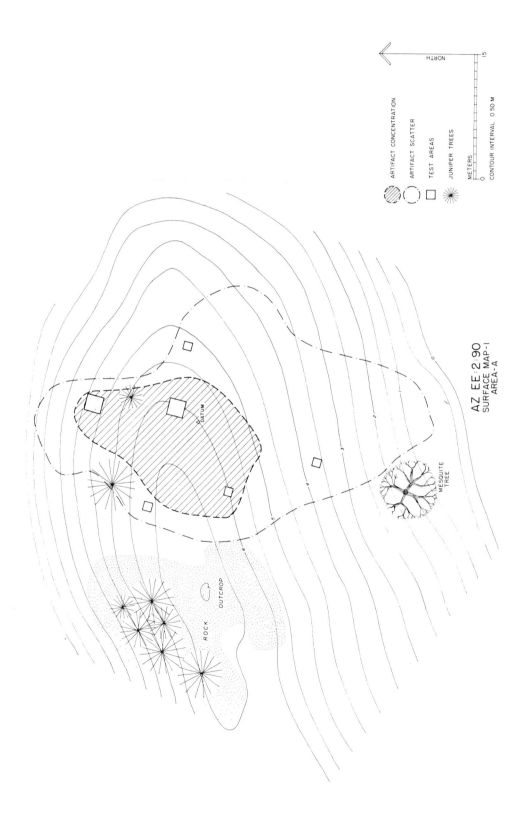

AZ EE:2:90
SURFACE MAP-1
AREA-A

ARTIFACT CONCENTRATION

ARTIFACT SCATTER

TEST AREAS

JUNIPER TREES

METERS

CONTOUR INTERVAL 0.50 M

NORTH

DATUM

MESQUITE
TREE

ROCK
OUTCROP

Figure 1.2   Map of AZ EE:2:90, Area A.

Only six units were included in the analyzed sample because of
the time-consuming nature of the attribute observations that were made.
In order to reduce the size of the sample, one-quarter of each of the
2-m-by-2-m units was analyzed. The remaining 1-m-by-1-m square from the
dense concentration, as well as the three units from the lighter density
scatter, was also included in the analyzed sample.

The depth of the cultural material in the test squares varied
from 10 cm below ground surface in the light density scatter to as deep
as 40 cm below surface in the densest concentration. Excavations were
terminated when sterile subsoil, consisting of a calcareous, gravelly
stratum, was reached.

Area B

The silicified limestone outcrop at Area B, located
approximately 100 m west of Area A, extends for a distance of 62 m from
the top of a hillcrest down the length of its south flank (Fig. 1.3). A
dense concentration of flakes of about 70 square meters is located on
the crest of the hill, and a lighter density scatter of flakes covering
approximately 1500 square meters extends southward down the hillslope
along the outcrop (Fig. 1.3). Artifact density ranges from 79 artifacts
per square meter in the densest concentration to approximately 68
artifacts per square meter in the lighter scatter, with an overall
density of approximately 71 artifacts per square meter.

The material from this outcrop differs somewhat from that of
Area A. It has a lighter gray color on fresh surfaces and patinates to
a white color. The material from Area B, like that of Area A, is
characterized by internal planes of natural fracture.

A single 1-m-by-1-m test square was excavated in the densest
part of the artifact scatter at Area B as part of the 1979 testing
project. Two additional 1-m-by-1-m squares were excavated in the dense
concentration, and seven more such units were excavated in the lighter
concentration during the 1982 mitigation project. Of the nine units
excavated at Area B, seven were judgmentally chosen to be included in
the analyzed sample.

Test squares were excavated to sterile subsoil, which was dark
brown, unconsolidated silt with orange outcrops of decomposing bedrock.
Depth of the cultural material in the units extended to 10 cm below
ground surface in the densest concentration and varied from 5 cm to
20 cm below ground surface in the lighter scatter.

A few artifacts recovered from AZ EE:2:103, a Late Archaic
habitation site excavated earlier in the mitigation phase of the
project, demonstrated that these people were utilizing material from the
silicified limestone quarry. A few flakes, a biface, and an incipient
biface all composed of the material which outcrops at Area B, were found
at this site. Further, two smaller, nearby Archaic sites (AZ EE:2:81
and AZ EE:2:87) also yielded a few flakes and cores of Area A silicified
limestone, documenting use of that source as well. These artifacts

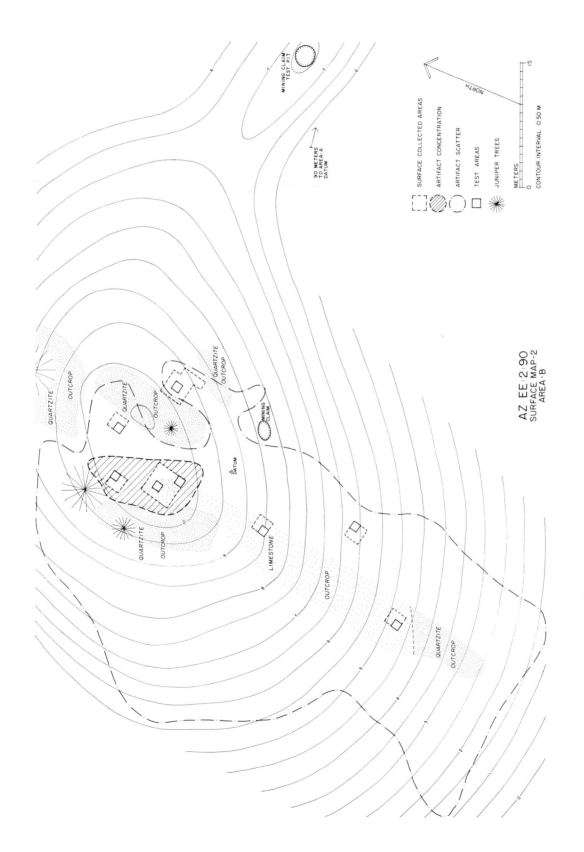

Figure 1.3 Map of AZ EE:2:90, Area B.

constitute a very small percentage of the total artifact assemblage from the sites, so the silicified limestone outcrops at AZ EE:2:90 were not a major source of lithic raw material for these Archaic people. Even so, the presence of these artifacts does give an indication that the Archaic inhabitants of the area knew of the material available at AZ EE:2:90.

Silicified limestone was also being used by some of the later ceramic period inhabitants of the Rosemont Area. Analysis of chipped stone material from these sites indicated that silicified limestone was present at most of them, making up 15 to 30 percent of the flaked stone assemblage. It was most abundant at four sites (AZ EE:2:76, AZ EE:2:84, AZ EE:2:105, and AZ EE:2:113), and several projectile points and other tools that were recovered were made of this material. In fact, silicified limestone represented the third most common material type found at the ceramic period sites. However, much of this was a black limestone found in cobble form throughout the Rosemont area. This suggests that although the silicified limestone from AZ EE:2:90 was utilized, it was not exploited extensively by the ceramic period people of the area.

AZ EE:2:131

AZ EE:2:131 is located on the flat top of a north-south trending ridge between Barrel Canyon and South Canyon (Fig. 1.1). The south end of the ridge is connected to a relatively high hill, which offers a vantage point from which a large area can be viewed. At the toe of the ridge are a number of limestone, quartzite, and granitic bedrock outcrops, consisting of a series of beds tilted on end and offset by a minor fault. Quartzite cobbles are abundantly strewn over the surface of the ridge, and a few metasediment cobbles are scattered over the south end of the ridge. It was these cobbles and, perhaps to a lesser extent the outcrops of quartzite that were being utilized for flaked stone artifact manufacture by the prehistoric inhabitants of the Rosemont Area.

The ridge supports elements of both desert grassland and woodland communities. Though dominated by dense areas of grasses, scattered over the ridge are several mesquite and juniper trees with some prickly pear and gray thorn. Recent human disturbance is indicated by a small rock cairn, probably a mining claim marker. Some cattle disturbance was also observed.

A low density scatter averaging approximately two artifacts per square meter and consisting of medium-grained quartzite flakes is located at the toe of the ridge. Within the scatter are five discrete knapping loci of the same material. At the opposite (south) end of the ridge, where it joins the hill, is a moderately dense concentration (three artifacts per square meter) of metasediment flakes and one discrete knapping feature composed of the same material (Fig. 1.4). As will be discussed in a later section, the discrete features and the artifact scatters were treated as separate samples for the purposes of the analysis.

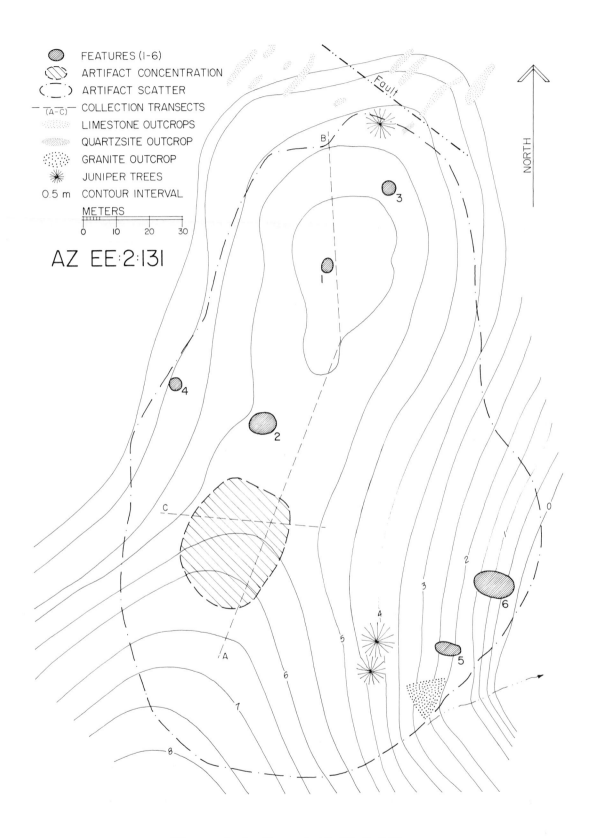

Figure 1.4 Map of AZ EE:2:131.

A contour map of the site was drawn using a plane table and alidade. It was felt that the chance of finding significant amounts of subsurface material at this site was small, based on the low artifact density and the geomorphology of the land surface on which the site is located. Therefore, the investigations at this site consisted of a controlled surface collection of artifacts rather than subsurface excavations. The surface collection was accomplished by laying out three selectively placed transects through the artifact scatters. Together, these three transects totaled 105 m in length by 1 m in width, and artifacts were collected from each 1-m-by-1-m unit along the transects. In addition, some retouched pieces that were found outside the limits of the transects were collected. Finally, the six discrete chipping features were mapped, and three of them (one composed of metasediment and two composed of quartzite) were completely collected.

Although the quartzite has a markedly coarser texture than the silicified limestone from AZ EE:2:90, it flakes readily and produces keen-edged, durable flakes. As such, it could have been used as a source of flakes for cutting tools, or for the manufacture of heavy duty tools such as choppers or scrapers. A few bifaces of quartzite were also found on the Archaic and Hohokam habitation sites in the project area.

The quartzite scatter is made up of large, unmodified flakes, many of them having cortex on the exterior surface. Only one retouched piece of this material, a crude uniface, was found at AZ EE:2:131. Of the six discrete knapping loci, the smallest was a scatter of 12 gray quartzite flakes, while the largest concentration contained about 450 purple quartzite flakes.

Feature 1, a relatively large concentration of flakes, was completely collected and attempts were made to reassemble the material. Although some flake groups were refitted, it became clear that many flakes as well as the core(s) were, in fact, missing. In view of the fact that this feature and Feature 4 are located on the relatively flat crest of the ridge, it seems unlikely that the missing flakes were removed by sheetwash or other natural causes. This suggests that the flintknappers kept some of the flakes as well as the cores or core tools, either for use or for further reduction elsewhere.

Two other discrete quartzite chipping features are located on AZ EE:2:131. Feature 6, which was also collected, consisted of two cores and a concentration of about 40 gray quartzite flakes within a 2.5-m-by-4.5-m area. A number of the flakes from this feature were reassembled onto the cores, one of which is a single platform core and the other of which had been flaked from two directions. The cores were probably part of a single cobble that was split in half, after which the broken face served as a platform for flake removal. In the case of the bidirectional core, the core face was later used as a second striking platform. In both cases, however, the cores could have been further reduced had the knapper chosen to continue. As with Feature 1, a number of flakes from two cores were missing, although the location of the feature on the steep margin of the ridge makes it possible that natural causes were, in part, responsible.

The last quartzite knapping locus, Feature 2, is the largest. It consists of two boulder cores embedded in the ground, two smaller cobble cores, a crude, unifacially retouched piece, and a dense concentration of approximately 450 flakes, all of the same purple quartzite. Two hammerstones were located within the boundaries of the feature, which covers a 3-m-by-4-m area. A feature of this size probably represents the activities of a number of flintknappers visiting the site at different times. This feature was mapped and photographed, but was not collected.

In addition to the quartzite artifacts, there is a moderately dense concentration (three artifacts per square meter) of artifacts composed of a gray to greenish-gray metasediment with small white speckles. This material is slightly coarser than the silicified limestone from AZ EE:2:90, and is characterized by fewer natural fracture planes. The material flakes more regularly than the silicified limestone, and can be employed for the manufacture of a wide variety of implements. The metasediment concentration is about 250 m in diameter and only slightly overlaps the quartzite scatter (Fig. 1.4), so that the two scatters are physically separate for the most part. A linear collection transect was run through the concentration in order to sample it.

In addition to the concentration of flakes, 17 retouched pieces of this metasediment and 1 of quartzite were collected. Some of these also exhibit use-wear, showing that they are not simply products of attempts to assess the suitability of the raw material. This suggests that the activities represented here were performed using tools manufactured on the spot from locally available raw materials.

Only one discrete knapping feature consisting of metasediment flakes (10) was found. This feature is located on a steep portion of the eastern margin of the ridge. Most of the flakes were reassembled, but they constitute only a small portion of the original core from which they were removed.

AZ EE:2:135

AZ EE:2:135 is situated on a north-south trending ridge jutting off the south side of an isolated, conical hill that forms the highest prominence in the immediate area (Fig. 1.1). Unlike most of the ridges in the area, this one slopes steeply towards the south along its entire length, and very little flat area is present along its crest. The ridge is composed of quartzite outcrops which are badly fractured and tilted, and which exhibit east-west strikes. The ridge top and slopes have a liberal cover of medium- and coarse-grained quartzite and a few fine-grained metasediment cobbles. It was these cobbles which were being exploited, not the bedrock outcrop. A low density cover of flaked stone artifacts (approximately two artifacts per square meter) litters the head of the ridge near its junction with the steep hill. The limits of the scatter are irregular, but they encompass an area approximately 70-m-by-30-m (Fig. 1.5).

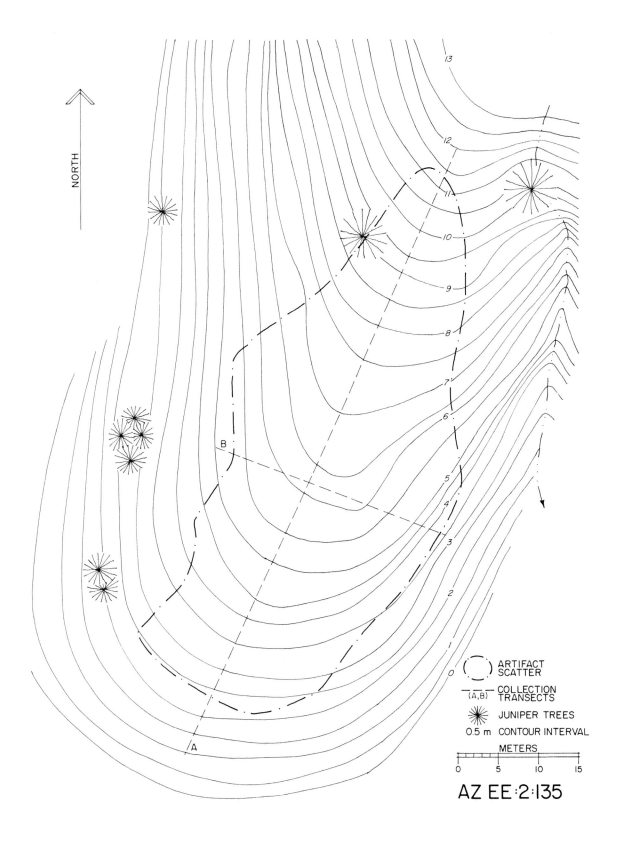

Figure 1.5 Map of AZ EE:2:135.

The ridge supports elements of both the desert grassland and oak woodland communities, and has a ground cover dominated by grasses. Prickly pear, mesquite, juniper, yucca, and bear grass are scattered throughout the site area. The mesquite grows in clumps on the ridge and is attractive to cattle, which have extensively disturbed the surface of the site. Recent human disturbance is minimal, and consists of a few small rock cairns on the edges of the ridge, which probably represent claim markers.

The collection strategy at AZ EE:2:135 consisted of establishing two surface transects, one 80 m long parallel to the long axis of the ridge, and one 30 m long perpendicular to the first. Artifacts were collected within 1-m-by-1-m units along the selectively placed transect. Retouched pieces from outside the transects were also collected, and a contour map of the site was drawn with a plane table and alidade.

The artifact assemblage at AZ EE:2:135 is made up mostly of quartzite flakes and cores, with a small percentage (about 15 percent) of metasediment debitage. Only five retouched pieces were found at the site. The nature of the artifact assemblage from AZ EE:2:135 suggests that, aside from lithic raw material reduction, a very limited range of other activities were carried out at the site.

In addition to the sites discussed thus far, five lithic material procurement sites were investigated in 1979 during the testing phase of the ANAMAX-Rosemont Project. Although the results of this work have already been reported (Huckell 1980), summaries will also be presented here in order to provide a basis for comparison with the other quarry sites. One of the five sites tested in 1979 was AZ EE:2:90, described above. Of the remaining four sites, three are small, low-density scatters of flaked stone material with from one to three discrete knapping features. The last site, AZ EE:2:89, is by contrast one of the largest lithic quarry sites in the area. Unfortunately, this site (as well as the others listed below) was removed from the land exchange area when the eastern boundary was redrawn after the testing phase. For this reason, no further work was undertaken there.

X85-S1-L1 and X85-S3-S1

These two localities were visited during the testing project, but were found to be so sparse that they were not mapped or collected, nor were ASM site numbers assigned to them. Both localities consist of very light scatters of flakes covering large areas of east-west trending ridges. One discrete knapping feature, representing the reduction of a gray quartzite boulder "macro-core," was found at X85-S3-S1. Three other such knapping features were identified at X85-S1-L1. The first of these also consisted of flakes struck from a single large core, and represents the reduction of a grayish green boulder "macro-core." The other two features were small clusters of unmodified flakes composed of from three to five different materials, each concentrated around several cores (Huckell 1980: 216-217).

Such low-density artifact scatters are quite common throughout the area because of the widespread occurrence of flakable quartzite, metasediment, and silicified limestone cobbles on the ridgetops around Rosemont. The potential of such localities to further our understanding of quarrying activities in the area is limited, but as a group they do show the opportunistic nature of the lithic material procurement activities in the area. Potentially useful materials were apparently tested for suitability wherever they happened to be encountered by the prehistoric knappers.

AZ EE:2:91

AZ EE:2:91 was found to be a much smaller, slightly more substantial artifact concentration than the preceeding two, and was investigated in more detail for that reason. The site is located outside the present eastern boundary of the land exchange area, on a ridge originating from the north slopes of a large, prominent escarpment against which Davidson Canyon heads (Fig. 1.1). It is covered with cobble to boulder gravels containing granite, limestone, quartzite, chert, metasediment, and conglomerate (Huckell 1980: 213). Three discrete knapping features and a few isolated artifacts were found on the ridge crest over an area measuring 75 m north-south by 15 m east-west (Fig. 1.6). The scatter of artifacts was quite sparse, amounting to only less than 0.2 artifacts per square meter.

The site was mapped with a tape and one of the knapping features was collected. It was tested with a single 0.5-m-by-1.25-m test unit excavated to a depth of 10 cm through the center of one of the features. This feature consisted of 1 hammerstone, 4 cores, and 41 flakes of chert, and 3 quartzite cores (Huckell 1980: 213). All these material types occur on the ridgetop. The two uncollected features consist of one concentration of 12 quartzite flakes in a 2.3-m-by-1.3-m area, with a possible associated core 5 m away, and a second small cluster of rhyolite chunks scattered around a large rhyolite boulder. This may not be a cultural feature, for the chunks showed no conclusive signs of having been worked. Although the total quantity of material at AZ EE:2:91 is small enough to have been quickly produced by one person in a short period of time, it could also have been produced during several visits over a long period of time. This type of site, along with X85-S1-L1 and X85-S3-S1, represents one extreme of flaked stone manufacturing activities around Rosemont, the very casual utilization of raw materials in the form of cobbles and boulders that were readily available on ridgetops throughout the area (Huckell 1980: 216).

AZ EE:2:89

AZ EE:2:89 also represents the use of raw materials available in cobble form, but is quite different from the smaller quarry sites. The site is located on a high, flat-topped ridge just west of State Route 83 (Fig. 1.1) which is composed of boulder gravels in a matrix of sandy

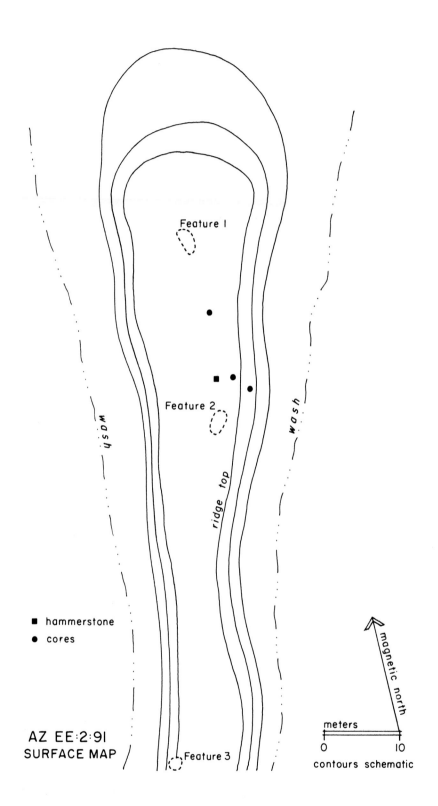

Feature 1

■ hammerstone
● cores

AZ EE:2:91
SURFACE MAP

Feature 2

ridge top

wash

wash

magnetic north

meters
0   10
contours schematic

Feature 3

Figure 1.6   Map of AZ EE:2:91

alluvium (Huckell 1980: 199-206). Quartzite and metasediment cobbles
suitable for flintknapping are present among the boulder gravels. The
top of the ridge is covered by a general scatter of flakes, and contains
26 discrete concentrations of flaked stone artifacts as well. The area
of the artifact scatter is about 300 m north-south by 30 m east-west,
considerably larger than the previously described sites (Fig. 1.7).

Most of the discrete concentrations represent single event
reductions of quartzite and metasediment boulder or cobble "macro-cores"
(Huckell 1980: 201). Twenty-two features consist of from one-to-five
large cores in association with varying numbers of large flakes that
have been removed from them. The other four features consist of "flakes
and cores of a variety of materials and a more normal size range"
(Huckell 1980: 201). Since these contain as many as 14 distinct raw
material types, they probably represent multiple-event knapping
features. A number of raw materials were identified among the artifacts
from AZ EE:2:89 including quartzite, metasediment, and smaller amounts
of silicified limestone, chert, and rhyolite. Two of the features from
AZ EE:2:89 were investigated: one single event cluster was completely
collected, and one multiple event cluster was sampled with transect
collection. The other features were mapped and their contents were
recorded.

Summary

Based on these investigations, two different kinds of quarry
sites can be distinguished in the Rosemont area. The first type,
represented only be AZ EE:2:90, is characterized by the exploitation of
large quantities of material occurring in bedrock outcrops, in this case
silicified limestone. The second and far more abundant type of quarry
consists of those sites which document the utilization of cobbles and
boulders secondarily deposited in alluvium (Fig. 1.8). These may range
from very small to very large loci. At one extreme are five sparse
sites (AZ EE:2:91, X85-S1-L1, X85-S3-S1, AZ EE:2:131, and AZ EE:2:135)
that represent the casual utilization of boulder gravels which occur on
ridges throughout the area. These gravels include abundant amounts of
quartzite cobbles as well as lesser amounts of metasediment, chert, and
silicified limestone (Huckell 1980: 198). AZ EE:2:89 represents the
somewhat more extensive utilization of boulder gravels. However, the
amount of material at AZ EE:2:89 is much less than is present at the
large silicified limestone quarry.

Analysis

In this section the analysis of the flaked stone debitage and
retouched pieces from the quarry sites is presented. The material
recovered during the testing phase of the project was not included in
the analysis, because the samples from AZ EE:2:89 and AZ EE:2:91 were
too small to allow statistically meaningful conclusions to be reached,

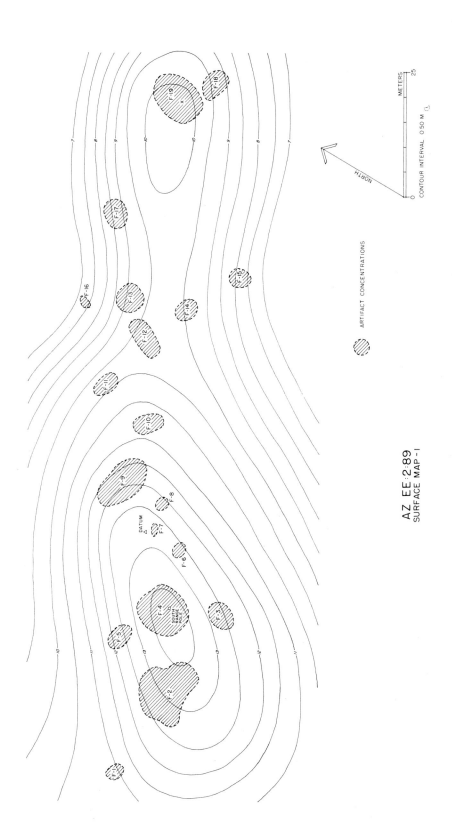

AZ EE:2:89
SURFACE MAP - I

Figure 1.7 Map of AZ EE:2:89, part 1

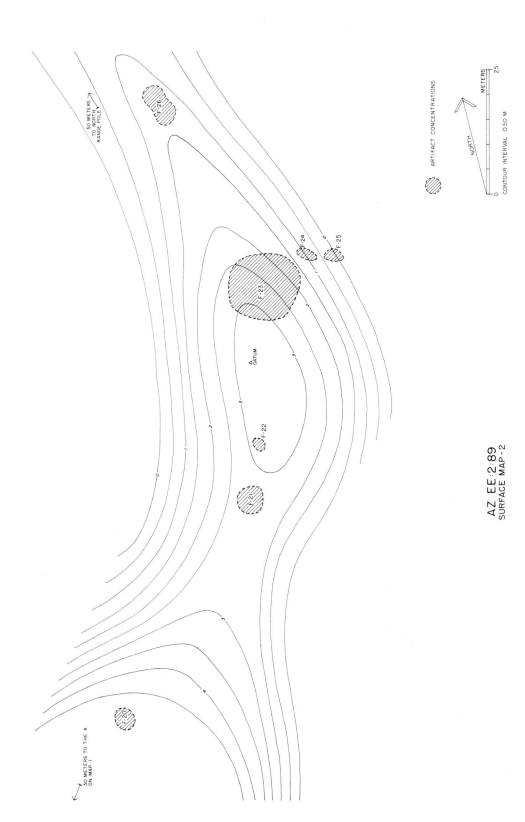

AZ EE:2:89
SURFACE MAP-2

Figure 1.7 Map of AZ EE:2:89, part 2

a

b

Figure 1.8 Two types of lithic raw material procurement sites. a, view of the
surface of AZ EE:2:90 Area B, a bedrock source of silicified limestone. The
light colored rocks are pieces of worked and unworked material adjacent to the
outcrop. b, view of the surface of AZ EE:2:131, a cobble and boulder source for
quartzite and metasediment. The light colored rocks are flakes, cores, and
boulders of quartzite.

and because an adequate sample of material was already obtained from the mitigation phase work at AZ EE:2:90. The first part of this section outlines the research objectives of this study, and is followed by presentation of the theoretical assumptions which underlie the work. The five samples from the sites that were used in the analysis are then defined, and the methodology used in the analysis is described. Next, the results of the analysis are presented, and in the last section the samples are compared to one another.

Research Objectives

Four research objectives were addressed in this study. The first objective was to describe the formal characteristics of the assemblages from the lithic quarry sites, and to identify differences among the assemblages. First, we were interested in differences in the characteristics of the debitage. Variability in such attributes as artifact type, flake size, amount of cortex, type of striking platform, and several other characteristics were taken into account. Second, differences in the assemblages of retouched pieces were also studied.

The second objective was to identify those types of activities other than lithic material procurement which might have occurred at the quarry sites. It was felt that such information would help to clarify the nature of these sites, even if no other kinds of activities could be detected.

The third objective was to distinguish the degree to which these sites were being utilized by Archaic period groups as opposed to Ceramic period groups. We attempted to accomplish this by studying techno-logical attributes of retouched pieces in the assemblages and by observing differences in the degree of patination on the artifacts. We also examined artifacts manufactured of local material that were recovered from the Archaic and Ceramic period habitation sites.

The fourth objective was to use discrete, single-event knapping features as a source of information about the lithic material procurement activities of the inhabitants of the area. Because the sites investigated during the mitigation project had far fewer such features than those visited during the testing phase, less information on discrete knapping features was obtained than had been expected. Nevertheless, by refitting flakes to several of the cores found at AZ EE:2:131, some specific information on the kinds of core reduction activities being conducted at this site was obtained.

Definitions and Assumptions

Any archaeological analysis is based on a set of assumptions made by the researcher in an attempt to make sense of the real world. Rozen (1979: 212-223, 1981: 162-165) has stated a number of assumptions concerning variability in the characteristics of debitage assemblages.

Those ideas which figured importantly in this analysis are summarized here.

Primary reduction is defined as the reduction of previously unaltered pieces of raw material (Rozen 1981: 162). The products include cores, flakes (both whole and broken), and shatter. The purposes of primary reduction are either to produce a tool by shaping the core itself, or to produce flakes which can then be used with or without additional modification. The modification of flakes after their removal from a core is an example of secondary reduction. Secondary reduction produces retouched pieces, flakes (both whole and broken), and shatter. Although the main qualitative difference between the products of the two types of reduction is the presence of cores as opposed to retouched pieces, other differences may also be apparent. It is assumed that primary reduction produces larger flakes with a greater proportion of complete flakes than secondary reduction. However, more intensive primary reduction will also produce smaller, less cortical flakes, so other characteristics of the debitage, such as the type of striking platform, can also help to distinguish between secondary and intensive primary reduction.

It should be remembered that the qualitative differences between primary and secondary reduction hold true only if all other variables remain constant. Variation in raw material, for instance, can have an important effect on the characteristics of debitage assemblages. If the size of the cobbles of given material is limited by natural fracture planes, the initial size of cores available for flaking will be small. This will result in the production of smaller, more cortical flakes, and can also result in a greater emphasis on the production of core tools through primary reduction, since the small size of flakes limits secondary reduction (Rozen 1979: 219-220).

The flaking characteristics of the raw material can also affect the debitage that is produced. Lower quality material will result in a greater proportion of shatter and irregularly shaped flakes. Moreover, the flaking characteristics of the rock may constrain the kind of reduction attempted by the flintknapper. For instance, coarse-grained material, because it is less suited to extensive secondary flaking, might be flaked exclusively by hard-hammer percussion, possibly with a certain task or specific tool in mind. In this instance technological variation would be the result of a deliberate choice by the flintknapper, based on constraints imposed by the limitations of the raw material and the desired product.

It is assumed that the way a site is used will also affect the character of the artifact assemblage. Sites that were revisited over a long period of time will have assemblages characterized by more intensive or extensive reduction. After much of the available material has been exploited, old cores and flakes may be reworked until they are unsuitable for additional reduction. These same results would be expected if a given raw material were in short supply or in high demand.

A final set of factors that can affect artifact assemblages has to do with natural processes and archaeological recovery techniques.

Sites located on a steep slope may be affected by sheetwash, resulting in movement of artifacts. Small artifacts will be affected to a greater degree than large artifacts. Also, small artifacts are less likely to be recovered than large artifacts in surface collection activities, even by trained archaeologists. All the sites are located on relatively similar geomorphological features, although, AZ EE:2:90 Area B and AZ EE:2:135 are located on steeper slopes than the other sites. Uniform recovery techniques were employed at all sites in order to minimize this source of bias.

Samples

A total of five samples of artifacts from the three sites investigated during the mitigation phase were compared in the formal analysis. AZ EE:2:90 was separated into two samples which were drawn from the two distinct areas of the site (Areas A and B), in order to examine variability between them. A total of 1263 artifacts from ten 1-m-by-1-m test squares were collected at Area A, and 1074 artifacts from six 1-m-by-1-m test squares were used in the sample. Four test squares were eliminated, two from each of the two 2-m-by-2-m units that were dug. Of the two pits from the 2-m-by-2-m units that were chosen to excavate, one was chosen randomly, and the other was picked judgmentally because it had been excavated deeper than the other units.

A total of 1902 artifacts from eight 1-m-by-1-m test squares were recovered from Area B, and 1434 artifacts from seven of the test squares were included in the analysis.

AZ EE:2:131 was also divided into two separate samples. The first consists of 227 artifacts collected from the surface along three 1-m-wide transects. The second is made up of 145 artifacts from three discrete knapping features that were collected. Justification for separating the features into a different sample rests not only on the fact that they represent discrete lithic reduction events, but also in that they consist primarily of quartzite, while the material from the transects is largely metasediment.

The assemblage from AZ EE:2:135 makes up the fifth sample, which includes all 129 artifacts collected from the surface of the site along the two 1-m-wide transects.

Analytical Methods

The formal analysis of the flaked stone artifacts recovered from the quarry sites consisted of measuring each artifact, and then recording additional information on a series of variables. These variables included provenience material type, artifact type, platform type, amount of cortex, and the presence or absence of platform, lipping, retouching, microflaking, polishing, striations, battering, abrasion, and patination (Table 1.1). Pieces of flaked stone that were

Table 1.1

LITHIC ATTRIBUTES RECORDED

Provenience
  ASM site number
  North-south grid coordinate
  East-west grid coordinate
  Transect or area
  Grid quarter
  Field number
  Feature number
  Stratum
  Level

Material type
  Quartzite
  Silicified limestone
  Limestone
  Basalt
  Rhyolite
  Chert
  Jasper
  Chalcedony
  Quartz
  Obsidian-pitchstone
  Mudstone
  Metasediment
  Igneous
  Metamorphic

Artifact type
  Complete flake
  Split flake
  Proximal flake fragment
  Medial-distal fragment
  Shatter
  Retouched piece
  Core
  Core-hammerstone

Measurements (to nearest mm)
  Length
  Width
  Thickness
  Maximum dimension

Platform type
  Cortical
  Plain
  Faceted
  Indeterminate
  Unidirectional
  Bidirectional
  Multidirectional

Retouching
  Absent
  Present

Lipping
  Absent
  Present

Cortex
  Complete flakes
    0%
    0-10%
    10-50%
    50-90%
    90-100%
  Broken flakes
    Absent
    Present
  Cores
    0%
    Less than 50%
    More than 50%

Use wear (present or absent)
  Microflaking
  Polishing
  Striations
  Battering
  Abrasion

Weight (cores; measured to
  nearest gram)

Patina
  Absent
  Present

retouched were subjected to additional observations and were classified as to type (Table 1.2).

All information was encoded on IBM FORTRAN coding forms, and was then keypunched on Hollerith cards and processed on the Central Data Corporation Model 6400 computer at the University of Arizona Computer Science Center. Statistical manipulation of the data was performed using the SPSS subroutine FREQUENCIES (Nie and others 1975).

The values that each variable could take were defined according to a consistent set of criteria in order to attain the greatest possible degree of replicability. In the following pages, each variable that was used in the debitage analysis is defined. Afterwards, the variables used in the analysis of retouched pieces are described.

Raw Material

Material type was noted for all classes of artifacts. Seven types of raw material were found to occur at the lithic quarry sites, although only three of these types occurred in significant quantities.

Silicified Limestone

Limestone is extremely common throughout southeastern Arizona, and magmatic events which occurred after its deposition sometimes metamorphosed it by impregnating it with silica. Silicified limestone occurs as bedrock outcrops at AZ EE:2:90, as well as in cobble form on ridges throughout the Rosemont area. Two separate outcrops having slightly different lithologic properties are located adjacent to one another at AZ EE:2:90. The material at Area B is light gray and is heavily flawed by fracture planes. The material at Area A is dark gray and is also heavily flawed. The material from both outcrops is fine- to medium-grained, and it often flakes well, provided that a piece relatively free of fracture planes can be found. However, because so much of the material contains flaws that affect its quality, a large number of pieces must be tested in order to obtain one that can be flaked precisely.

Quartzite

Quartzite occurs on many ridgetops throughout the area, both in cobble form and as outcrops. However, the material that is suitable for flintknapping is concentrated in the area east of Barrel Canyon (Fig. 1.1). Grain size varies from coarse to medium and, although the quartzite is significantly coarser than the other materials found at the lithic quarries, it can be flaked without difficulty. Color also varies, ranging from gray to green to purple. The chief advantage of this material is that it is plentiful and occurs in cobbles of larger size than do the other material types. As such, it would have been a suitable material for the production of larger tools such as choppers or large scrapers, and flakes of this material would also have served as efficient and durable cutting or scraping tools.

Table 1.2

OBSERVATIONS MADE ON RETOUCHED PIECES

Attribute	Values
Artifact type	Flake
	Core
	Chunk
	Indeterminate
	Split cobble
	Cobble
Artifact size	Small retouched piece
	Large retouched piece
Retouch type	Unifacial
	Bifacial
Retouched piece type	Scraper
	Denticulate
	Irregularly retouched piece
	Miscellaneous flaked chunk
	Miscellaneous unifacially retouched piece
	Bifacially retouched piece
	Projectile point
	Chopper
Scraper type	End
	Side and transverse side
	Multisided
	Undifferentiated
	Discoidal-ovoid
	Side-end
	Interior surface
Wear pattern	Battering
	Polishing
	Microflaking
	Striations
	Microflaking and polishing
	Indeterminate
	None
Patination	Present
	Absent

Metasediment

Metamorphosed sediments are common throughout the Rosemont area. They are basically indurated mudstones and siltstones, produced by metamorphic processes akin to those that produced the silicified limestone. They come in a wide variety of textures ranging from fine to coarse. Colors are extremely variable, including green, gray, brown, red, and purple. All the different varieties have light-colored speckles throughout the material. Metasediment occurs at AZ EE:2:131 in cobble form, and is available in the same general area as the quartzite. The material is generally slightly coarser than the silicified limestone and natural fracture planes are prevalent, so that pieces available for reduction are small and covered with cortex. Even so, this material flakes predictably, and the finer grade is perhaps more suited to bifacial reduction than the silicified limestone. A wide variety of metasediment material occurs at the Archaic and Hohokam habitation sites, and much of it was probably obtained from different outcrops in the foothills of the Santa Ritas.

Other Materials

Fewer than half a dozen flakes each of rhyolite, chert, mudstone, and limestone were found at the lithic quarry sites. Because the frequencies of these materials are so low, they will not be described in detail here.

Artifact Type

Eight classes of artifacts were established for the purpose of analyzing the typological composition of the flaked stone assemblages from the quarry sites.

Complete Flake

All flakes that were whole, or which were only broken in places that did not interfere with taking accurate length, width, and thickness measurements, were classed as complete flakes.

Split Flake

Flakes that split longitudinally from the point of percussion of the striking platform to the distal end of the flake were included in this category. Since no width measurements could be made on these flakes, only maximum size was measured.

Proximal Flake Fragment

Flakes in which all or part of the platform was intact, but which lacked the distal or lateral edges were included in this category. Maximum size was recorded on proximal flake fragments.

Distal and Medial Flake Fragment

Flake fragments in which the striking platform and possibly one or more lateral or distal edges were missing were included in this category. Maximum length of these fragments was recorded.

Shatter

All irregular, angular fragments of debris on which the interior and exterior flake surfaces could not be distinguished were classified as shatter. Maximum size was recorded.

Retouched Piece

Retouched pieces are those that have been reduced by the removal of a series of flakes along one or more edges. No attempts were made until a later stage in the analysis to distinguish between intentionally produced retouch and edge damage due to accidental factors.

Core

Cores are pieces from which flakes have been struck, and which could not themselves be identified as flakes. Secondary cores, flakes from which other flakes have been removed, were classified as retouched pieces at this stage of the analysis and were sorted out later. Cores were weighted, maximum size was measured, and the direction of flaking was noted as described in the following discussion of platform type.

Core-Hammerstone

This class of artifacts includes any core exhibiting battering which appeared to be a result of use as a hammerstone. These pieces have crushed and rounded platform margins and a globular shape.

Platform Type

In cases where an intact striking platform was present on a flake, it was classified into one of five categories. This information was recorded because it was believed that differences in the type of platform might represent differences in the kinds of lithic reduction strategies being employed. Four types of striking platforms were established for flakes.

Cortical

Platforms which consisted entirely or partially of the nodular cortex were included in this category.

Plain

Platforms with a featureless, noncortical surface were classified as plain platforms.

Faceted

Platforms exhibiting portions of two or more flake scars on their surfaces were classified as faceted platforms.

Indeterminate

Flakes or flake fragments that clearly show the point of impact on the interior surface but which lack the actual striking platform as a result of shattering or crushing were included in this category.

Platform type was also recorded for cores. Three categories were established, based on the number of platforms from which flakes originated. Although the definitions used are theoretically distinct, in actuality there were times when the classification of a given artifact was difficult, because most of the cores at the quarry sites were irregularly shaped pieces on which it was often hard to determine the origins of the flake scars.

Unidirectional

Cores having a single set of platforms, with flake scars all running in the same direction were classed as unidirectional cores.

Bidirectional

Cores having two separate sets of striking platforms, with flake scars running along two different core faces were classed as bidirectional cores.

Multidirectional

Cores with flake scars originating from three or more striking platforms and traveling along three or more faces of the core were called multidirectional cores.

Cortex

The amount of cortex was noted for all artifacts. Complete flakes were separated into five categories based on the relative quantity of cortex on the exterior surface of the flake and platform. The five categories were: no cortex, 1-10 percent cortex, 11-50 percent cortex, 51-90 percent cortex, and 91-100 percent cortex. On flake fragments, only the presence or absence of cortex was noted. On cores, cortex was divided into three categories: no cortex, less than 50 percent cortex, and greater than 50 percent cortex. The percentage of cortex on a flake or core was estimated by visual examination of the artifact; no devices for measuring the amount of cortex were used.

Lipping

All flakes with whole or partial platforms were also checked for the presence of lipping, which is commonly associated with the soft hammer percussion manufacture of bifaces. A lip is defined as an overhang of the striking platform on the interior surface of the flake. If the lip was not pronounced, it could be detected by running a fingernail along the interior surface against the platform.

Patination

At both areas of AZ EE:2:90, obvious differences could be detected in the degree of patination exhibited by the flakes that were recovered. In order to obtain some measure of the degree to which these sources were being exploited by Archaic period groups as opposed to Ceramic period groups, the presence of patina was recorded. However, an artifact was only included in the patinated category if a relatively thick, almost chalky layer of patina was present. Although it was recognized that this was subjective and would be difficult for another researcher to replicate, it was felt that this would give some indication of the relative amounts of use by Archaic and Hohokam populations. A significant proportion of the flakes exhibited a very light patina.

Later on, when the debitage analysis of the Archaic sites was underway, a few artifacts manufactured of the silicified limestone at AZ EE:2:90 were identified at two Archaic sites, one dating to the Middle Archaic and one to the Late Archaic. It was found that on some of these pieces, the degree of patination was considerable, even at the Late Archaic site. However, one broken biface recovered from the Late Archaic site exhibited only a slight degree of patina and would have been classified as unpatinated in this system. It may be that the material from Area A does not patinate at the same rate as that of Area B. It is also possible that the rate of patination differs between subsurface artifacts and those exposed on the surface, and microenvironmental differences among sites may also affect patination rates. Therefore, the results of these measurements should be viewed with caution. Although we remain confident that our observations do offer a reasonable indication of relative age between populations of artifacts,

individual pieces of contemporaneous age may vary from one another
depending on the factors discussed above.

A thick, chalky patina such as described above did not occur on
the quartzite or metasediment artifacts. The metasediment did sometimes
develop a thin patina, but this tendency was so slight that it was felt
that any attempt to classify these artifacts would be highly subjective.

Other Attributes

Observations were made on a number of additional attributes
relating to modification of the artifact either intentionally or through
use. Retouching was defined as the removal of flakes from the margin of
the artifact, and its presence was recorded. Microflaking, defined as
the removal of a series of very small flakes (less than about 3 mm in
length and width), was also recorded. It was differentiated from
retouching in the belief that this microflaking results from use.
Although a number of methodological problems immediately present
themselves regarding the ability to distinguish between small retouch
flakes and large use-wear flakes, it was not the purpose of this study
to address such issues. Moreover, the number of retouched and utilized
pieces recovered from the quarry sites was small enough that no problems
were encountered in classifying these assemblages.

The presence or absence of abrasion along the juncture between
the striking platform and the exterior surface of the flake was also
recorded. This kind of abrasion, which was detected by examination
using the naked eye or a hand lens, is presumably the result of
preparation of the striking platform for flake removal.

The presence or absence of polishing, defined as a sheen or
luster occurring along the margin of a tool, was also recorded.
Polishing was often accompanied by edge attrition, defined as the
removal of small amounts of material from the edge, resulting in
rounding and dulling of flake margins.

The presence or absence of striations, small, shallow scratches
along the edge of a tool, were also recorded. Striations frequently
occurred with polish. The recording system was set up so that the
categories were not mutually exclusive and more than one category of
wear could be recorded for a given artifact.

Flake Dimensions

In addition to recording various nonmetric attributes, all
artifacts were measured to the nearest millimeter using Vernier
calipers, in order to examine dimensional characteristics of the
assemblages. Length, width, and thickness were recorded on complete
flakes. Length was measured on the interior surface of the flake, from
the point of impact to the farthest point on the distal end of the
flake. Width was measured perpendicular to length at the midpoint of
the length dimension. Thickness was measured as the maximum distance

between the interior and exterior surface at the longitudinal midpoint of the flake. This measurement differs from that which is sometimes used (for example Leach 1969; Rozen 1979, 1981), a fact that should be taken into consideration if these measurements are compared to other sets of data.

For the various categories of broken flakes, measurements of length, width and thickness could not be taken. Therefore, only the maximum dimension was recorded for these categories of artifacts.

Retouched Pieces

All retouched pieces from the lithic quarry sites were subjected to additional study with the purpose of identifying the possible functions of the pieces, and as a result gaining a clearer understanding of the kinds of activities being performed at the sites. In addition to classifying the retouched pieces as to type, both the kind of retouch (bifacial or unifacial) and the nature of the wear patterns were recorded. Table 1.2 lists all the observations that were made on the retouched pieces.

Artifact Size

Retouched pieces were divided into two general categories based on the size of the artifact. Large retouched pieces are those greater than 80 mm in maximum dimension, including pieces manufactured on cobbles, cores, and large flakes. Small retouched pieces are less than 80 mm in maximum dimension, and include pieces made on smaller flakes, pieces of shatter, and natural pebbles.

Retouch Type

Two categories were established for recording the kind of retouch which was present. Unifacially worked pieces were those which had been flaked on one face of the artifact from a single striking platform surface, while bifacially worked pieces had been flaked on two faces from opposing surfaces.

Retouched Piece Type

All retouched pieces were next classified as to type. The classification system that was devised includes seven commonly used artifact types. Although many of the terms used to designate these types carry functional implications, such implications are not necessarily intended for the artifacts from the quarry sites, since the study of patterns of use-wear indicates that many of the retouched pieces were not actually used as tools. Instead, these categories are intended to describe the gross morphology of the artifacts.

Scrapers. The largest category of retouched pieces recovered
from the quarry sites were scrapers. These objects are typically
manufactured on flakes, the interior surface of which serves as the
striking platform for the removal of a series of retouch flakes from the
opposite face. The unifacial edge thus created could have served a
variety of purposes. Because of the considerable amount of
morphological variation among the scrapers, they were subdivided into
several subtypes: end scrapers, retouched along the distal end of the
flake; side scrapers, retouched along one lateral edge; transverse side
scrapers (which are morphologically similar to side scrapers) also have
retouching on the long margin of the flake, but in this case it is the
distal end; undifferentiated scrapers, retouched to the extent that the
striking platform has been removed; discoidal or ovoid scrapers,
retouched along the entire margin of the piece; side-end scrapers,
retouched along both a lateral edge and the distal end; and interior
surface scrapers, those that have been retouched on the interior surface
of the flake.

Denticulates. Like scrapers, denticulates have a unifacially
flaked edge, but are distinguished by the tooth-shape of the margin.
Denticulates display a series of more widely-spaced, deeper flakes,
creating a broad, serrated edge. Two kinds of denticulates were
recognized. The first has had a series of large, deep flakes removed,
probably by percussion, to create a sharp, serrated edge. The second
kind is similar to the first, except that the margin was then pressure
flaked to create a more undulating edge.

Irregularly Retouched Pieces. This category, which is the
second most numerous type recovered from the quarry sites, is made up of
a diverse set of artifacts. These are characterized by an irregular
retouch in which a small number of nonoverlapping flake scars are
present along several different edges. It is most likely that these
pieces were not intentionally retouched to form tools, but rather have
been accidentally damaged.

Miscellaneous Unifacially Retouched Pieces. These pieces are
characterized by unifacial retouch, but were not classified into one of
the more formal categories such as "scrapers" or "denticulates" for one
of several reasons. Some of these pieces have only been worked along a
small portion of an edge, while others show a less regular pattern of
retouching than the scrapers or denticulates. These pieces do, however,
appear to have been intentionally rather than accidentally produced, and
they probably represent attempts by flintknappers to assess the
suitability of a particular piece of stone for further reduction.

Bifacially Retouched Pieces. This category includes several
small, thick, bifacially flaked artifacts in which the retouch is
neither very refined nor very extensive, again suggesting that the
knappers were testing the suitability of these pieces for further
reduction.

Projectile Points. Projectile points are small bifaces, usually with extensive retouch over both faces, which have commonly been modified in some way to facilitate hafting. Two projectile point fragments were recovered from the quarry sites.

Choppers. Choppers are defined as large, heavy, bifacially flaked artifacts made on large flakes or cores. Two choppers were recovered.

Wear Patterns

In an attempt to determine how many of the retouched pieces had actually been utilized and to what purposes they were being put, each was examined with a 10 power hand lens for evidence of use. Several categories of use-wear were recognized. Battering, which occurred on hammerstones, was defined as crushing, pitting, and rounding of the edges of a cobble. Polishing was defined as a sheen or luster along the margin of a tool, and it was often accompanied by edge attrition. Microflaking was a series of small flakes (less than about 3 mm in length or width) removed from the edge of an artifact, presumably as a result of use. Striations were defined as sets of small, shallow scratches along the edge of a tool. A category which included both microflaking and polishing was established in order to accomodate tools that had this combination of wear patterns. The final categories included one in which no use-wear was present on the artifact, and one in which use-wear could not be distinguished due to the development of heavy patina on the artifact.

Patina

The last variable that was recorded for retouched pieces was the presence or absence of patina. As with the debitage, this observation was only made on silicified limestone artifacts. Only those pieces which exhibited a substantial development of patina, resulting in an overall white to whitish-gray chalky covering, were recorded as having patina.

Data Presentation and Comparisons

In this section, information on the nature of the artifact assemblages of the three quarry sites will be presented, and the five samples will be compared and contrasted to one another. As mentioned earlier, Areas A and B at AZ EE:2:90 were treated as separate samples because they are physically separate and because of slight differences in the lithologic characteristics of the raw material at each area. The features and transects from AZ EE:2:131 were also treated as distinct samples, because they are made up of different raw material types. Finally, the artifacts from AZ EE:2:135 were analyzed as a single sample. These samples form the basic units of comparison.

Raw Material

Table 1.3 gives the frequency of occurrence of lithic material type among the five samples. Both areas at AZ EE:2:90 are made up almost exclusively of silicified limestone, with a very small amount of quartzite (consisting of a fraction of a percent from each area). The nonfeature material from AZ EE:2:131 is predominately metasediment, with a noticeable amount of quartzite, as well as small quantities of rhyolite, chert, and mudstone. In contrast, the features at AZ EE:2:131 as well as the sample from all of AZ EE:2:135 yielded mostly quartzite, with small amounts of metasediment. It will be suggested that many of the differences among the lithic quarry samples are based on differences in raw material. Although the small number of samples available for comparison makes it difficult to evaluate this contention, the significant differences in the qualities of these material types probably account for much of the observed variation.

Artifact Type

Table 1.4 shows the frequencies of artifact types among the samples, while Figure 1.9 presents these figures graphically. Once again, the two areas at AZ EE:2:90 display similar frequencies, although Area A shows a lower incidence of whole flakes and a higher incidence of distal and medial fragments. The material from AZ EE:2:135 shows a higher frequency of whole flakes than the other sites, and a considerably lower frequency of distal and medial fragments. The sample from this site and the features at AZ EE:2:131 have a higher frequency of split flakes. Nonfeature material from AZ EE:2:131 has the highest frequency of both shatter and retouched pieces, while the features from this site have the lowest frequencies of those types. The sample from AZ EE:2:135 and the nonfeature material from AZ EE:2:131 have a higher frequency of cores than the other samples. Interpretations of these differences will be offered in a later section.

Platform Type

Table 1.5 gives the frequencies of platform types for flakes, while Table 1.6 does the same for cores. Surprisingly, the two samples from AZ EE:2:90 differ noticeably in this attribute. Area B has almost twice as many cortical platforms. AZ EE:2:135 also has a high frequency of cortical platforms, with no faceted platforms. The nonfeature material from AZ EE:2:131 has a high frequency of indeterminate platforms, while the sample from the features at this site has a very low percentage of cortical platforms but high frequencies of plain and faceted ones.

With the exception of AZ EE:2:90, the samples of cores from the quarry sites are too small to derive many conclusions. The two samples from AZ EE:2:90 do not show any marked differences, although Area A has a slightly higher frequency of bidirectional cores than Area B, and consequently has fewer unidirectional and multidirectional cores.

Table 1.3

MATERIAL TYPE FREQUENCIES

Provenience	Silicified Limestone	Quartzite	Rhyolite	Chert	Mudstone	Metasediment	Limestone	Total
AZ EE:2:131 transects		38 (17.0)	2 (1.0)	3 (1.0)	2 (1.0)	182 (80.0)		227
AZ EE:2:131 features		136 (94.0)				9 (6.0)		145
AZ EE:2:135 transects	110 (85.0)					18 (14.0)	1 (1.0)	129
AZ EE:2:90 Locus A	1073 (99.8)	2 (0.2)						1075
AZ EE:2:90 Locus B	1432 (99.9)	2 (0.1)						1434

( ) = percent

Table 1.4

ARTIFACT TYPE FREQUENCIES

Provenience	Whole Flakes	Split Flakes	Proximal Fragments	Medial-Distal Fragments	Shatter	Retouched Piece	Cores	Total
AZ EE:2:131 transects	74 (33)	9 (4)	28 (12)	49 (22)	35 (15)	15 (7)	17 (7)	227
AZ EE:2:131 features	50 (34)	21 (14)	23 (16)	45 (31)	3 (2)	1 (1)	3 (2)	146
AZ EE:2:135 transects	51 (40)	17 (13)	25 (19)	16 (12)	9 (7)	2 (1)	9 (8)	129
AZ EE:2:90 Locus A	274 (26)	56 (5)	159 (15)	487 (45)	48 (4)	21 (2)	29 (3)	1074
AZ EE:2:90 Locus B	454 (32)	71 (5)	223 (16)	559 (39)	49 (3)	22 (2)	56 (4)	1434

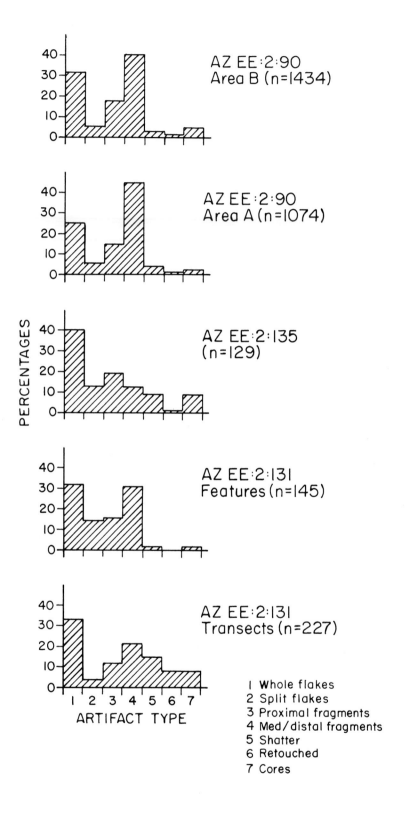

Figure 1.9 Artifact type frequencies for all samples.

Table 1.5

FLAKE PLATFORM TYPE FREQUENCIES

| Provenience | Platform Types | | | | Total |
	Cortical	Plain	Faceted	Indeterminate	
AZ EE:2:131 transects	41 (26.3)	71 (45.6)	4 (2.5)	40 (25.6)	156
AZ EE:2:131 features	10 (10.2)	75 (76.5)	8 (8.2)	(5.1)	98
AZ EE:2:135 transects	39 (39.8)	54 (55.1)		5 (5.1)	98
AZ EE:2:90 Locus A	118 (20.8)	350 (61.8)	29 (5.1)	69 (12.2)	566
AZ EE:2:90 Locus B	324 (40.0)	385 (47.6)	21 (2.6)	79 (9.8)	809

Table 1.6

CORE PLATFORM TYPE FREQUENCIES

	Platform Type			
Provenience	Unidirectional	Bidirectional	Multidirecional	Total
AZ EE:2:131 transects	8 (42.1)	9 (47.4)	2 (10.5)	19
AZ EE:2:131 features		1 (50.0)	1 (50.0)	2
AZ EE:2:131 quartzite	4 (36.4)	4 (36.4)	3 (27.2)	11
AZ EE:2:135 transects	4 (44.5)	3 (33.3)	2 (22.2)	9
AZ EE:2:90 Locus A	9 (31.0)	17 (58.6)	3 (10.4)	29
AZ EE:2:90 Locus B	22 (39.3)	26 (46.4)	8 (14.3)	56

( ) = percent

Cortex

Tables 1.7, 1.8, and 1.9 give the frequencies of the various categories used to describe cortex on complete flakes, flake fragments, and cores. Figure 1.10 presents the information on whole flakes as a series of bar graphs. AZ EE:2:135 has the highest percentage of flakes with less than 50 percent cortex. The two areas at AZ EE:2:90 differ somewhat, with the flakes at Area A tending to have less cortex, and those from Area B more cortex. The feature and nonfeature samples at AZ EE:2:131 are relatively similar, although the transect sample has slightly higher quantities of flakes with more cortex.

Interestingly, when the information from broken flakes is used as the basis for comparison, the ranking is changed (Table 1.8). However, if the information on the amount of cortex on whole flakes is converted to presence or absence (that is, flakes having no cortex and those with cortex), the rankings conform more closely to the results derived from the observations on broken flakes. It should be pointed out that much information is lost when only presence or absence of cortex is considered, and the observations on whole flakes are probably a more accurate measure of the degree of cortex in an assemblage.

Lipping

Figures on the frequency of lipping are not presented, since all the five samples had less than 1 percent lipped flakes.

Patination

The frequency of patination was only recorded for the two areas at AZ EE:2:90, for only the silicified limestone displayed obvious differences in this trait. Area A has twice the amount of patinated artifacts with 25 percent (266 of 1074 artifacts) compared to 12 percent in Area B (166 of 1434 artifacts). This may be the result of more extensive use of Area A material earlier in the Archaic period, or may be a result of natural causes such as a difference in the patination rate of the material from the two areas.

Flake Dimensions

Figures 1.11 through 1.13 illustrate the length, width, and thickness curves for the whole flakes in the samples, and Figure 1.14 gives the maximum size curves for the flake fragments in the same samples. Because thickness measurements cluster together more tightly and have less absolute variance than do other variables, differences among the samples are more easily identified by comparing the curves for this variable.

The thickness curves for whole flakes from AZ EE:2:90 Areas A and B (Fig. 1.13) are very similar, as might be expected given the similarity in raw material type, and presumably in the kinds of lithic

Table 1.7

COMPLETE FLAKE CORTEX FREQUENCIES

			Percent Cortex			
Provenience	0	1-10	11-50	51-90	>90	Total
AZ EE:2:131 transects	25 (28.4)	16 (18.2)	31 (35.2)	14 (15.9)	2 (2.3)	88
AZ EE:2:131 features	17 (32.0)	9 (17.0)	22 (41.5)	3 (5.7)	2 (3.8)	53
AZ EE:2:135 transects	19 (31.7)	24 (40.0)	13 (21.7)	4 (6.7)		60
AZ EE:2:90 Locus A	126 (45.2)	31 (11.1)	74 (26.5)	42 (15.1)	6 2.2)	279
AZ EE:2:90 Locus B	133 (29.2)	77 (16.9)	127 27.9)	81 (17.8)	38 (8.3)	456

( ) = percent

Table 1.8

CORTEX FREQUENCIES FOR FLAKE FRAGMENTS

| | Cortex | | |
Provenience	Present	Absent	Total
AZ EE:2:131 transects	90 (73.8)	32 (26.2)	122
AZ EE:2:131 features	43 (47.8)	47 (52.2)	90
AZ EE:2:135 transects	32 (54.2)	27 (45.8)	59
AZ EE:2:90 Locus A	332 (42.7)	435 (57.3)	775
AZ EE:2:90 Locus B	493 (53.5)	429 (46.5)	922

( ) = percent

Table 1.9

CORTEX FREQUENCIES FOR CORES

| | Percent Cortex | | | |
Provenience	None	Less than 50	More than 50	Total
AZ EE:2:131 transects	2 (11.8)	12 (70.6)	12 (17.6)	17
AZ EE:2:131 features		2 (100.0)		1
AZ EE:2:135 transects	2 (20.0)	7 (70.0)	1 (10.0)	10
AZ EE:2:90 Locus A	6 (20.7)	17 (58.6)	6 (20.7)	29
AZ EE:2:90 Locus B	9 (16.1)	36 (64.3)	11 (19.6)	56

( ) = percent

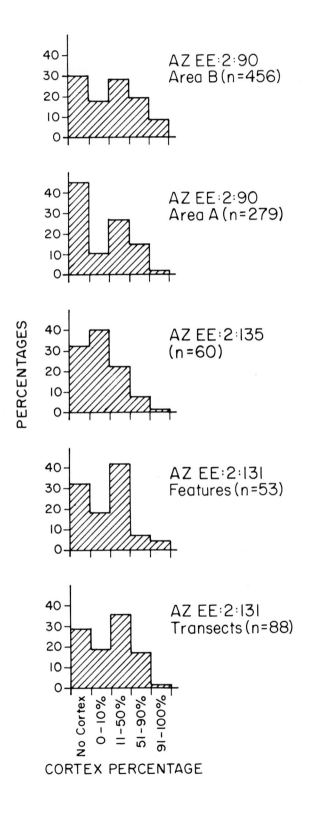

Figure 1.10   Cortex frequencies for all samples.

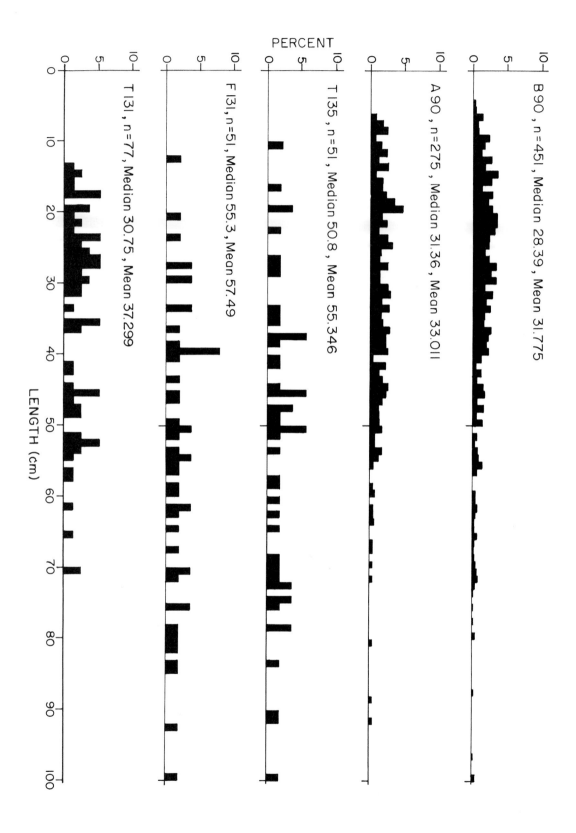

Figure 1.11   Flake length frequencies for all samples.

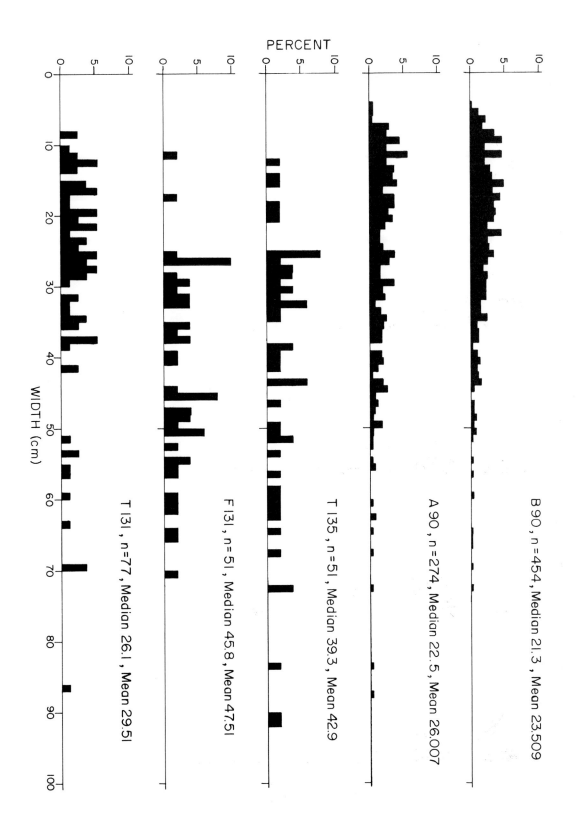

Figure 1.12   Flake width frequencies for all samples.

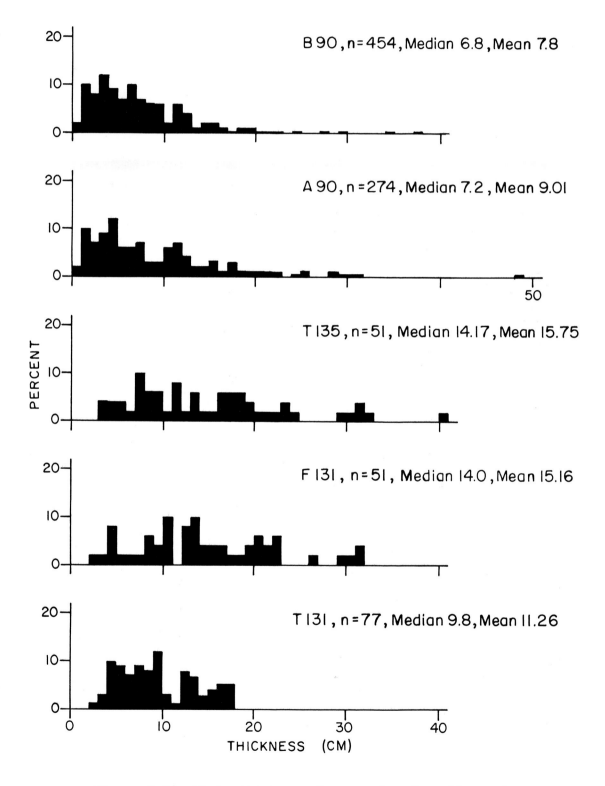

Figure 1.13   Flake thickness frequencies for all samples.

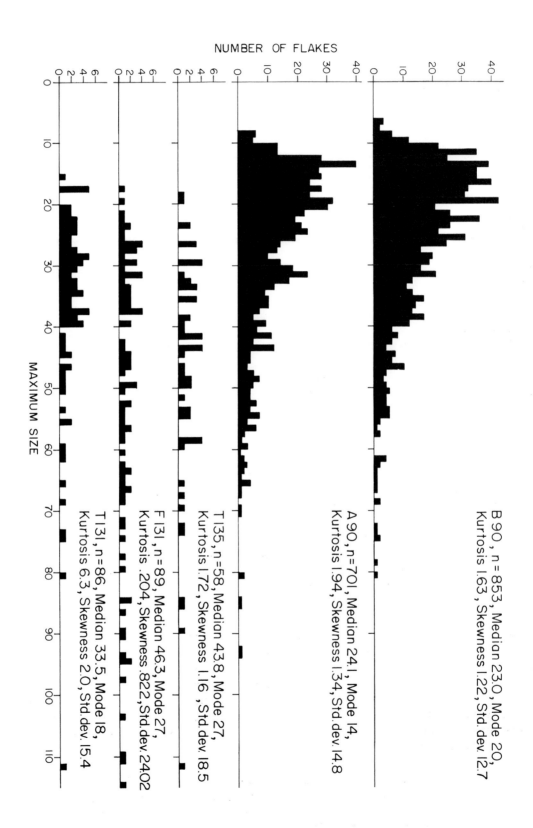

Figure 1.14   Maximum size frequencies for broken flakes from all samples.

reduction activities undertaken at these loci over an extensive period of time. These two samples have peaked curves, are skewed to the left, and have smaller medians than the other assemblages. They do differ somewhat in that the whole flakes from Area A are slightly but consistently larger, not only in thickness, but length and width as well. The thickness curves for the AZ EE:2:135 sample and the feature sample at AZ EE:2:131 are also similar to one another, and have considerably larger medians than the curves for the other samples. This is probably due to the fact that both samples are composed primarily of quartzite, which occurs naturally in larger pieces and has a coarser texture. These factors could result in the production of larger and thicker flakes. The thickness curve for the AZ EE:2:131 nonfeature material is dissimilar to all the other curves. It is slightly skewed to the left, but has a more rounded peak than the curves for the two samples from AZ EE:2:90.

The length and width curves (Figs. 1.11 and 1.12) follow this same trend. The curves for both areas of AZ EE:2:90 are very similar, having peaks that are skewed to the left with small medians. The length and width curves of flakes from AZ EE:2:135 and the features at AZ EE:2:131 are again similar to each other, but differ from the two AZ EE:2:90 samples in that they consist of longer and wider flakes. The nonfeature material from AZ EE:2:131 differs from all the other flake curves in that it has a tighter peak. As with the thickness curves, the type of lithic material being flaked seems to be the main factor in the similarities and differences in flake size.

Retouched Pieces

Table 1.10 gives the frequencies of retouched pieces at the quarry sites, and Figures 1.15 and 1.16 illustrate some of the implements from AZ EE:2:131 and AZ EE:2:135. Figure 1.15 illustrates a selection of retouched pieces form AZ EE:2:131. These retouched pieces, all but one of metasediment, are better constructed than those from the other samples, displaying more uniform, careful retouching. Illustrated are three discoidal scrapers (Fig. 1.15 a-c), two side scrapers (items d and e), and two bifaces (items f and g).

The artifacts that contain this sample are not dissimilar from those found on some of the Archaic sites in the area (Huckell 1984), given the ovoid scrapers and small bifaces. It is possible that a small Archaic component was present here, in addition to the material relating to lithic procurement. Tools were being manufactured of the metasediment and quartzite that occurs on the site, and many of the tools were then put to use on the spot. This material probably represents a specialized brief Archaic occupation, perhaps for the purpose of exploitating floral or faunal resources in the area.

Five retouched pieces were found at AZ EE:2:135, and only two of these (constituting 2 percent of the assemblage) came from the randomly collected sample. The five pieces, probably Archaic, include two projectile point fragments (Fig. 1.16a and b), the fracture patterns of which suggest that they were broken, and perhaps lost during hunting.

Table 1.10

RETOUCHED PIECES FROM THE QUARRY SITES

Provenience	Scrapers	Denticulates	Irregularly Retouched Pieces	Miscellaneous Flaked Chunks	Miscellaneous Unifaces	Small Percussion-Flaked Bifaces	Projectile Points	Choppers	Provenience Subtotal	Total
AZ EE:2:131										
transects	8 (44.4)		7 (38.9)			3 (16.7)			18	19
features	1 (100.0)								1	
AZ EE:2:135										
transects	1 (20.0)						2 (40.0)	2 (40.0)	5	5
AZ EE:2:90										43
Locus A surface	3 (30.0)	1 (10.0)	5 (50.0)		1 (10.0)				10	
Locus A subsurface	5 (45.5)		4 (36.4)		2 (18.2)				11	21
Locus B surface	4 (40.0)		1 (10.0)	2 (20.0)	3 (30.0)				10	22
Locus B subsurface		1 (12.5)	3 (37.5)		3 (37.5)	1 (12.5)			8	
Locus B Feature 1	2 (50.0)	1 (25.0)	1 (25.0)						4	
Total	24	3	20	2	9	4	2	2		67

51

Figure 1.15 Retouched pieces from AZ EE:2:131. <u>a</u>-<u>c</u>, discoidal scrapers; <u>d</u>-<u>e</u>, side scrapers; <u>f</u>-<u>g</u>, bifaces.

Figure 1.16 Retouched pieces from AZ EE:2:135. a-b, projectile point fragments;
c-d , choppers.

The third artifact is an unifacially retouched piece that may have been used as a scraper. The remaining two pieces are large tools with heavy battering on the edges (Fig. 1.16c and d). They both appear to have been made on the same variety of quartzite, and were probably made on the spot for a specific purpose (such as collecting and processing fibrous plants, or woodcutting) and then discarded.

The two areas from AZ EE:2:90 have similar frequencies of retouched pieces (Table 1.10). Scrapers and irregularly retouched pieces make up the majority of these assemblages, but only 5 percent of the retouched pieces in assemblage have use-wear. Twenty-nine percent of the retouched pieces from Area A are patinated, twice the amount from Area B and, therefore, about the same as from the debitage samples.

Wear Patterns on Retouched Pieces

Fifty-six percent of the retouched pieces (10 of 18 artifacts) in the sample of nonfeature material from AZ EE:2:131 have observable wear. Eight of these have microflaking, one has microflaking and polishing, and one has polishing only. Although the sample from AZ EE:2:135 has a greater proportion of retouched pieces with use-wear, that amounts to only three out of five retouched pieces with wear. Two of the three worn tools are choppers which display battering on their edges, and the third tool, a scraper, displays polishing. The two samples from AZ EE:2:90 have very low frequencies of use-wear on the retouched pieces. Only 1 of 21 pieces from Area A had use-wear, in this case polishing. One of 22 pieces from Area B has discernable use-wear, in the form of microflaking. The single retouched piece found in the sample of material from the features at AZ EE:2:131 lacked use-wear.

Interpretations

Having presented and reviewed the data that were recorded for each sample of lithic quarry artifacts, it is appropriate now to attempt to interpret these data. In this section, important differences among the debitage and retouched pieces of the five assemblages will be discussed, in an attempt to identify the ways in which lithic raw materials were being exploited, and to identify other activities that are represented in the assemblages.

The material from AZ EE:2:135 is most similar to the assemblage from the features at AZ EE:2:131. The complete flakes from these samples are larger in all dimensions than those from the other samples, and the maximum dimensions of broken flakes are considerably larger. Also, both samples have significantly higher proportions of split flakes. It is suggested that these similarities are due to the properties of the raw material which are contained in these samples, for both of them are predominantly quartzite. The occurrence of larger flakes of this material can be attributed to two factors. First, because quartzite occurs as large cobbles which are relatively free of internal flaws, it is possible to produce larger flakes from this material. Second, the coarseness of the grain size of the quartzite found at these two sites would limit the kinds of reduction techniques that could be used, given that it would seem more logical to do finer, controlled flaking on fine-grained materials.

A further similarity between these two samples is the small size of the retouched piece assemblages that were recovered. Only a single retouched piece came from the features at AZ EE:2:131 (constituting 1 percent of the sample), a crude uniface from Feature 2. No use-wear is present on this piece, and it probably represents an attempt to assess the suitability of the material for secondary reduction. Five retouched pieces were found at AZ EE:2:135, and only two of these (constituting 2 percent of the assemblage) came from the randomly collected sample. The five pieces include two projectile point fragments, the fracture patterns of which suggest they were broken during hunting. The third artifact is a unifacially retouched piece that may have been used as a scraper. The remaining two pieces are large tools with heavy battering on the edges. They both appear to have been made of the same variety of quartzite, and were probably made on the spot for a specific purpose (such as collecting and processing fibrous plants, or woodcutting), and then discarded. Altogether, the small number of retouched pieces found in these two samples suggests that few activities other than lithic reduction were being carried out.

Despite the close similarities between the samples from the features at AZ EE:2:131 and AZ EE:2:135, some specific differences do exist. First, there is a much higher incidence of whole flakes and a lower incidence of flake fragments at AZ EE:2:135 compared to the features at AZ EE:2:131. Conversely, there is a lower incidence of cortical platforms and a higher incidence of plain and faceted platforms at AZ EE:2:131. All these trends are interpreted to result from the extent to which cores were reduced during the formation of the chipping features at AZ EE:2:131. A close scrutiny of the material from Feature 1 and Feature 6 (the two quartzite reduction events at AZ EE:2:131) indicates that both features resulted from extensive primary reduction of cores. In both cases, the cores have been reduced to the point that only flakes with plain or faceted platforms are being produced. The sample from AZ EE:2:135, on the other hand, seems to be the result of less extensive lithic reduction. The kinds of striking platforms in this sample suggest that many cobbles were being tested, but that more extensive core reduction seldom took place.

The nonfeature material from AZ EE:2:131 differs in several ways from the two samples discussed above and the two samples from AZ EE:2:90. First, the nonfeature sample from AZ EE:2:131 is composed primarily of metasediment. As previously mentioned, this material was observed during fieldwork to occur in the form of small, fractured pieces, which are frequently covered with cortex. The small size of the material is most likely the reason for the higher proportion of cortical flakes in the sample, since if only smaller cores are available for reduction, more cortical flakes will be present in the assemblage. Moreover, the highly fractured nature of the material may account for the higher proportion of shatter in the sample.

The nonfeature sample from AZ EE:2:131 also had high proportions of cores and retouched pieces. The retouched pieces, all of which are made of the locally available metasediment, are better made than those from the other samples, being more carefully and uniformly retouched. Also, more than 50 percent of the retouched pieces in the sample exhibit use-wear in the form of microflaking and polishing. The artifacts that make up this sample are not dissimilar from those found on some of the Archaic sites in the area (Huckell 1984), given the ovoid scrapers and small bifaces. It is possible that a small Archaic component was present here, in addition to the material relating to lithic procurement. Tools were being manufactured of the metasediment and quartzite that occurs on the site, and many of the tools were then put to use on the spot. This material probably represents a specialized Archaic component that was occupied for a brief period, perhaps for the purpose of the exploitation of floral or faunal resources in the area.

Not surprisingly, the two assemblages from AZ EE:2:90 resemble each other closely. Both silicified limestone outcrops at the site have been extensively exploited over a long period of time, as witnessed by the abundance of debitage. The material available at the site is not of exceptional quality, but the large volume of stone that was present probably served as an inducement for flintknappers to return to the site. Most likely, the vast quantities of waste flakes present at the two areas of the site were produced over the course of a long period of time, as suggested by the presence of varying degrees of patina on the material.

The two samples from AZ EE:2:90 have very similar flake size histograms (Figs. 1.11 through 1.14) and the artifact type frequencies also resemble each other closely (Table 1.4). The assemblages of retouched pieces from the two areas are virtually identical. All are made of the locally available silicified limestone. Most are unifacially retouched, and the extent of modification is limited. Wear patterns were noted on only one of the pieces from Area A and one from Area B. It is likely that most, if not all, of the retouched pieces were not made with the intent of producing tools, but rather to test the suitability of the pieces for secondary retouch. Virtually no evidence was recovered to indicate that activities other than lithic reduction occurred at the site.

Despite the overall similarities, some subtle differences between these two samples do exist, which is interesting in view of the close proximity of the two areas and the similarity in raw material. The sample from Area B has a higher incidence of partially and mostly cortical flakes, and fewer noncortical flakes. Also, the sample from Area B has a higher proportion of flakes with cortical platforms, and consequently, lower proportions of flakes with plain and faceted platforms. During the fieldwork, the material from Area A was observed to be somewhat less highly fractured than the material from Area B, which may account for the observed differences between the assemblages. If the material from Area A is not fractured as badly, larger pieces would be available for reduction, and the debitage assemblage would be expected to have less cortex. Also, the cores could have been more completely reduced before they were too small to conveniently handle, which would result in more flakes with plain and faceted platforms. The fact that the flake size curves of Area A are slightly larger than the sample from Area B in length, width, and thickness of whole flakes, and in the maximum size of flake fragments, may also be a function of the larger pieces at Area A.

Another difference between the two samples is the frequency of patinated flakes. Area A has twice as many patinated flakes (25 percent) as Area B (12 percent). Although it is possible that several factors including differing chemical or physical properties might cause variation in the rate of patination, the magnitude of the difference between the two areas suggests that Area A might also have been more extensively exploited during an earlier time. This is to be expected if the material from Area A has fewer flaws, since the earlier groups using the quarry might have preferred the better quality material. Later, as more of the material had been worked, the flintknappers would have made greater use of the less desirable material.

In conclusion, much of the variation among the samples can be attributed to differences in the lithic material being flaked. The samples most similar to one another are the two silicified limestone assemblages from AZ EE:2:90, and the two quartzite assemblages from AZ EE:2:135 and the features at AZ EE:2:131. Some variation can be attributed to the differences in the patterns of exploitation of bedrock outcrops as opposed to scattered cobbles and boulders. However, even though the sites produced by each of these two kinds of exploitative patterns are different in nature, the characteristics of the debitage assemblages showed very little variability. This is because the same activity, the primary reduction of cores, created both kinds of assemblages. The variability in the sample of nonfeature material from AZ EE:2:131 can be attributed to its specialized nature, in that the metasediment at this site was being used for tool manufacture, and the tools produced were put to use on the spot.

Conclusions

Investigations were carried out on three lithic material procurement sites in December 1982 as part of the ANAMAX-Rosemont Mitigation Project, as a followup to excavations done in 1979 as part of the ANAMAX-Rosemont Testing Project. These investigations attempted to provide some insights as to how the lithic procurement activities of the inhabitants of the Rosemont area were structured.

Analysis of the recovered artifactual material and comparisons of the individual quarry site revealed the opportunistic nature of lithic raw material procurement among the local inhabitants of the Rosemont area. Two types of quarry sites were identified during the projects: secondary cobble quarries and bedrock quarries. The first type is represented by three small localities visited during the testing phase, AZ EE:2:91, X85-S1-L1, and X85-S3-L1, and by the larger sites of

AZ EE:2:131, AZ EE:2:135, and AZ EE:2:89. The material present here represents the limited exploitation of cobbles which are present on ridges throughout the area. Such sites are quite common in the Rosemont area, due to the ubiquity of flakable cobbles throughout the area. These sites represent a very casual kind of lithic reduction activity, wherein different materials were tested for suitability as they were encountered in the course of the normal routine.

AZ EE:2:131 and AZ EE:2:135, lying only one quarter mile (0.4 km) apart, are examples of the same type of site. Although there is enough material present to suggest that they may have been visited more than once, the absolute amount of chipped stone is still very small. The quartzite and metasediment cobbles present at these sites were occasionally tested by flintknappers, perhaps in the course of other activities, but the sites were never the focus of intensive exploitation. AZ EE:2:131 and AZ EE:2:135 were more accessible than some of the other small quarry sites, since they are located within 1 mile (1.6 km) of 17 Hohokam habitation sites and 4 Archaic sites. In addition to lithic reduction, these small sites had evidence of other kinds of activities, including hunting and plant gathering.

AZ EE:2:89 is similar to the small quarry sites discussed above, since flakable cobbles and boulders were being exploited at this site. However, it differs in that the absolute amount of flaked stone material at AZ EE:2:89 is much greater than at the sites discussed above. The variety of material types found at this site is also greater, including not only quartzite and metasediment, but silicified limestone, rhyolite, and chert as well (Huckell 1980: 201). Twenty-six knapping features were identified at this site, four of which were made up of numerous raw material types. This site, therefore, represents the same kind of lithic exploitation as the sites discussed above, but on a larger scale.

In addition to their considerable variability in size and intensity of use, these secondary sources of cobbles and boulders also represent the majority of the lithic material procurement sites in the Rosemont area. As noted in the introduction, over 50 such localities have been recorded here, and it is probable that many others exist to the north and east of the present exchange area. In short, cobbles and boulders of quartzite, metasediment, chert, silicified limestone, and other materials are ubiquitous in the area, and afforded prehistoric flintknappers easy access when the need arose for lithic raw material.

AZ EE:2:90, by contrast, represents a qualitatively different kind of lithic quarry site. The amount of flaked stone material is considerably greater, since the silicified limestone occurs as large bedrock outcrops. Because of the quantity of material available for knapping, the inhabitants of the area would have returned to the site again and again. AZ EE:2:90 lies within 1 mile (1.6 km) of eight Hohokam sites and five Archaic sites. Although it is not suggested that any of these sites were specifically located so as to take advantage of the quarry, nevertheless, this source was clearly known to the inhabitants of the area. They visited it regularly, as shown by the massive quantities of debitage at the site itself, as well as by the

Chapter 2

THE SYCAMORE CANYON SITES

Martyn D. Tagg
Bruce B. Huckell

In 1981, as the direct result of the exclusion of seven square
miles of land on the eastern side of the original parcel of the
ANAMAX-Rosemont land exchange, it was proposed that an additional parcel
to the north of the then-current exchange boundaries be added to the
project area. This parcel consisted of 3.5 contiguous sections along
the northern boundary of the original exchange area (Fig. 2.1), and is
made up almost exclusively of the Sycamore Canyon drainage network.
Archaeological survey of the Sycamore Canyon parcel by CRMD
archaeologists located two prehistoric sites (Ferg 1981), which were
excavated during the mitigation phase of the ANAMAX-Rosemont Project.
The sites were originally thought to contain distinct preceramic and
ceramic components, but the excavations revealed a mixture of these
components, making identification of culturally distinct artifact
assemblages impossible. For this reason, and because the two sites lie
in a drainage system distinct from the Barrel Canyon system that drains
the Rosemont area, the results from the excavation of these sites are
treated separately rather than included in the Rosemont Archaic or
Hohokam reports (Huckell 1984; Ferg and others 1984). This report
presents descriptions of the two sites and a formal analysis of the
recovered artifacts, followed by a discussion of the cultural, temporal,
and functional aspects of the sites.

Environment

The Sycamore Canyon parcel is located at the extreme
northwestern end of the Santa Rita Mountains, separated from the main
exchange area by the high, northeast-trending ridge line of the range
(Fig. 2.1). The parcel consists primarily of the northern and southern
branches of the head of Sycamore Canyon, and is characterized by steep,
predominantly north- and west-facing mountain and ridge slopes dissected
and drained by narrow, deeply incised canyons (Ferg 1981: 3). The
bedrock underlying the ridges consists of both Tertiary-Cretaceous
volcanic rocks and Paleozoic limestone, with some metamorphosed

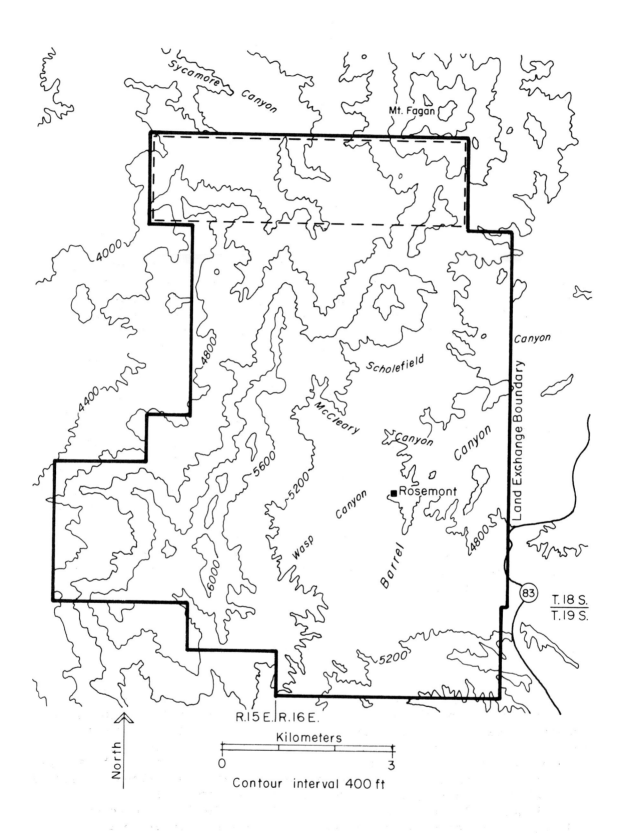

Figure 2.1 Location of the Sycamore Canyon parcel (enclosed by dashed line) in relation to the rest of the ANAMAX-Rosemont land exchange area.

limestone and granite. Lower ridge slopes, consisting mainly of cobble
and boulder alluvium from the erosion of the surrounding mountains and
isolated by recent drainages, represent the only relatively flat land in
the area (Ferg 1981: 3-5). The two prehistoric sites in the parcel are
located on these low ridge segments overlooking the northern branch of
Sycamore Canyon (Fig. 2.2). These low lying ridges support a desert or
semidesert grassland plant community which characterizes most of the
study area (Lowe 1981: 45). Very little of the original perennial grass
stands remain due to livestock overgrazing, range-fire suppression, and
climatic dessication. The entire Sycamore Canyon parcel has been used
for cattle grazing since at least 1937, which has paved the way for
nongrass "noxious plant invaders". This includes stands of mesquite
(Prosopis juliflora) which have invaded the area since the introduction
of cattle; shindagger (Agave schottii) occurring in extensive clusters
and constituting as much as 80 to 95 percent of the local cover in areas
where the former topsoil is gone; snakeweed (Gutierrezia sp.), burroweed
(Haplopappus sp.), buckwheat (Eriogonum fasciculatum), fairy-duster
(Calliandra eriophylla), and ocotillo (Fouquieria splendens). Other
common desert and desert grassland species such as agave, prickly pear
and other cacti (Opuntia spp.), Condalia, and scattered oaks also occur
(Lowe 1981: 45-51). Small remaining amounts of native perennial grasses
such as blue grama (Bouteloua gracilis) may be found throughout the
area. This vegetation is common between elevations of 4000 and 5500
feet, including most of the Sycamore Canyon parcel, which ranges in
elevation between 3840 and 5720 feet (Ferg 1981: 5). Precipitation
generally averages from 14 to 19 inches annually (Lowe 1981: 45).

Other plant communities present in the study area include the
riparian forest, evergreen woodland, and limestone scrub. Riparian
forest is found around springs and along the major canyon bottoms, and
consists of sycamore, walnut, hackberry, and cottonwood trees.
Evergreen or oak-juniper woodland is presently restricted to the higher
elevations directly above the canyons and is dominated by oak and
juniper. Finally, the limestone scrub community usually occurs at
higher elevations wherever limestone is exposed or is the substrate.
This community is dominated by oak, agave, mountain mahogany, sumac and
sotol, and also contains mariola (Parthenium incanum) and sandpaperbush
(Mortonia scabrella) common to Chihuahuan desertscrub communities (Lowe
1981: 54). The presence of these four plant communities in a relatively
restricted geographic area would have been advantageous for the local
inhabitants, and may be the reason the sites exist in Sycamore Canyon.

Various animal species are also present in Sycamore Canyon.
Twenty-three species of mammals were recorded in the area, with most
evidence seen around permanent water sources in the southern branch of
the canyon. The mammals include seven species of bats, desert
cottontail, black-tailed jack rabbit, rock squirrels, three species of
mice, woodrat, coyote, gray fox, ringtail cat, coatimundi, mountain
lion, whitetail deer, mule deer, and javelina. Most of those species
present are in low numbers due to the absence of grasslands, the steep
topography, and degradation by cattle overgrazing (Petryszyn 1981:
106-108; Hungerford 1981: 111). Fifty-seven bird species are known in
the Sycamore Canyon region, with the red-tailed hawk and Gambel's quail
the most commonly seen (Russell and Goldwasser 1981: 102). Also present

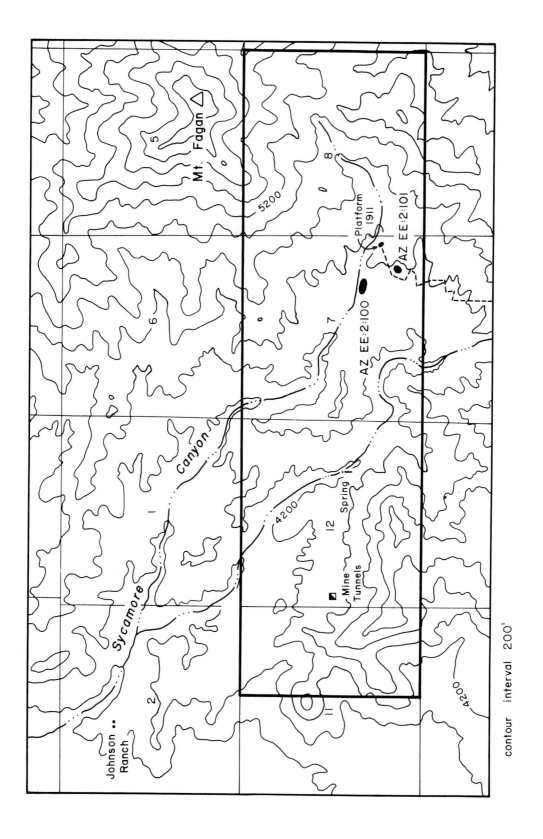

Figure 2.2   Locations of AZ EE:2:100 and AZ EE:2:101 in Sycamore Canyon.

are many species of reptiles, including the desert tortoise, 15 species
of lizards, and 20 species of snakes (Lowe and Schwalbe 1981: 92).   The
animals most commonly seen during the work at the two sites were
whipsnakes, blacktail rattlesnakes, and whitetail deer.

Site Descriptions

As may be seen from Figure 2.2, both of the sites are located in
the upper part of the north branch of Sycamore Canyon.   They are
separated from one another by a distance of only 200 m, although a high
ridge prevents a direct view of one site from the other.

AZ EE:2:100

AZ EE:2:100 is located on the basically flat top of an east-west
trending lower ridge at the base of a very rocky hill.   It is bordered
on the north, in part, by another short ridge remnant and by the deeply
cut north branch of Sycamore Canyon.   Another shallow tributary wash
runs south of the ridge, and joins Sycamore Canyon to the west of the
site (Fig. 2.3).   The surface of the site consists of a moderately
fine-grained alluvium with scattered cobbles and boulders.   The ridge
supports a desert grassland community dominated by a dense growth of
mesquite punctuated by lycium, burroweed, prickly pear, a few chollas,
and sparse annual grasses.   There is no evidence of recent human
disturbance; however, cattle grazing is evidenced by cow chips on the
site and occasional sightings of animals.

A moderately dense scatter of flakes covering the top of the
ridge and upper portion of the slopes marked the site, encompassing an
area approximately 40 m north-south by 80 m east-west.   In addition
there were three distinct surface features within the scatter
(Fig. 2.3).   The investigation strategy for this site was very similar
to that employed at the Archaic sites in the Rosemont area (Huckell
1984: 43-45).   A contour map was drawn using a plane table and
alidade but, due to the density of artifacts, no systematic surface
collections were made.   Instead, culturally or temporally diagnostic
artifacts were pinflagged, point-provenienced on the map, and collected.
A transit was used to create a basic grid system of 4-m-by-4-m squares,
aligned to magnetic north, which served as the basis for the selection
of grid squares to be excavated.   A combination systematic and random
sampling procedure was employed in which alternating rows of 4-m-by-4-m
grid squares were arbitrarily designated for sampling, within which
alternating grid squares were arbitrarily chosen, and a randomly
selected quarter (2-m-by-2-m square) of these squares was designated for
excavation.   To vary the sampling pattern, the arrangement of alternate
4-m-by-4-m squares was shifted arbitrarily from one row to the next.   If
features were located, or a sample square yielded a high subsurface
artifact density, selected contiguous grid squares would be excavated.
The excavation of the 2-m-by-2-m squares consisted of the removal of

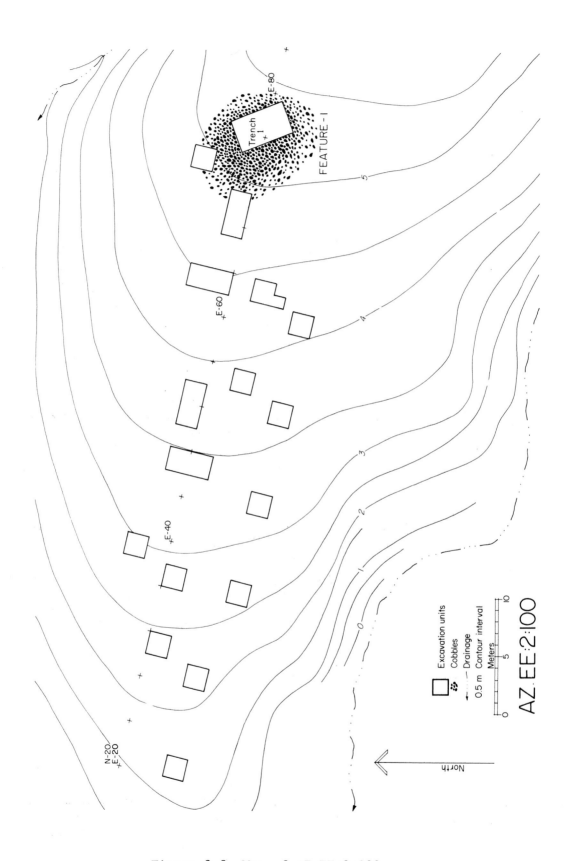

Figure 2.3 Map of AZ EE:2:100.

earth with shovels, picks, pick mattocks, and trowels in arbitrary 10-cm levels. All excavated earth was passed through a one-quarter inch mesh screen. When encountered, features were excavated as naturally defined provenience units. Artifacts recovered included ceramics, flaked and ground stone, and bone.

Features

Only three culturally constructed rock features were investigated at this site, and two of them were exposed on the surface. Both surface features consisted of roasting pits or fire cracked rock concentrations derived from roasting pits; the sole buried feature was a small hearth.

Feature 1

A moderately dense surface concentration of fire-cracked rocks covering a roughly oval 10-m diameter area on the main body of the site was labelled Feature 1. Scattered among the rocks were sherds, flaked and ground stone artifacts, and bone. A 5-m-by-3-m trench was excavated in the east half of the feature, with a dense concentration of fire-cracked rocks filling most of the trench. Further excavation through this first level of rock revealed scattered fire-cracked rocks to 60 cm below ground surface, most heavily concentrated at 30 to 40 cmbs. A few scattered ash lenses were also present (Fig. 2.4). Artifacts were recovered in every level, although the majority came from the first level. Sherds were found as deep as Level 5 (50 to 60 cmbs), suggesting that this is a Hohokam feature. While no actual pit was defined, the masses of rock that make up this feature are clearly derived from one or more nearby roasting pits.

Feature 2

Also in the main portion of the site and 5 m from Feature 1 is a small cluster of rocks, 75 cm by 110 cm in area, which probably represents one or two hearths (Fig. 2.5). The small- to medium-sized cobbles lay in two somewhat distinct circular concentrations, each approximately 75 cm in diameter. The cobbles of one of the concentrations appeared to be in a shallow, 15 cm deep pit, which was filled with a dark gray, charcoal-rich silt. Sherds and flaked stone artifacts found in the half that was excavated suggest that this feature belongs to the Hohokam occupation of the site. The second concentration may represent cleanout or disturbance from the tested hearth, or may be another hearth.

Feature 3

Located at the head of the short ridge remnant to the north of the main ridge was Feature 3, a large roasting pit. It was roughly circular (2 m in diameter) and consisted of large, fire-cracked boulders

Figure 2.4   Feature 1 at AZ EE:2:100 after definition.

Figure 2.5   Feature 2 at AZ EE:2:100 after definition.

Figure 2.6   Feature 3 at AZ EE:2:100 after definition.

Figure 2.7   Feature 3 at AZ EE:2:100 after partial excavation.

in a pit extending 50 cm below ground surface (Figs. 2.6 and 2.7). The
boulders remained densely packed within the pit, with charcoal and ash
scattered throughout the fill. Artifacts were scarce, consisting of a
few pieces of flaked stone, sherds, bone, and possibly burned agave.

AZ EE:2:101

AZ EE:2:101 is a small site, approximately 60 m north-south by
25 m east-west, situated on the eastern edge of a relatively flat,
northeast-southwest trending ridge. It is bordered on the south and
east by a fairly deep canyon incised into bedrock, and on the west by a
shallow drainage channel (Fig. 2.8). Bedrock, consisting mainly of
quartzite, is exposed to the west of the site and is near the surface of
the site itself, where the ground is covered with small angular rock
fragments. The ridge supports a desert-grassland community dominated by
a thick grove of small mesquites on the northern part of the site, and
including annual grasses, shindagger, burroweed, prickly pear, and
buckthorn. Recent human disturbance is minimal, represented by a few
pieces of historic trash (a vaccine bottle, two shotshell bases, one
piece of glass) and the mining access road 20 m to the northwest of the
site. Cattle grazing is in evidence.

A light scatter of flakes (less than one per square meter)
covers the side of the ridge, and three distinct surface features were
located within this scatter. The investigative strategy for this site
was the same as for AZ EE:2:100, except that all surface artifacts at
AZ EE:2:101 were point-plotted on the plane table map, and collected.
This was accomplished by crew members forming a line abreast of each
other and walking back and forth in transects paralleling the long axis
of the site. All artifacts found, including ceramics and chipped and
ground stone, were pinflagged for mapping and collection (Huckell 1984).
The grid system was set to parallel the long axis of the ridge rather
than magnetic north.

The selection of grid squares to be excavated at this site was
accomplished using the same procedure outlined for AZ EE:2:100.
However, because the squares chosen for excavation at AZ EE:2:101 proved
to have less than 10 cm of cultural fill in them, a great deal more of
this site was excavated. Excavation methods for this site were
identical to those employed at AZ EE:2:100.

Features

Three feature numbers were assigned to various culturally
produced rock concentrations, as seen at AZ EE:2:100. Two of these were
completely visible on the surface and one was encountered during
excavation. However, the two surficial features appear to represent
structural remains, and the buried feature is a fine example of a
roasting pit.

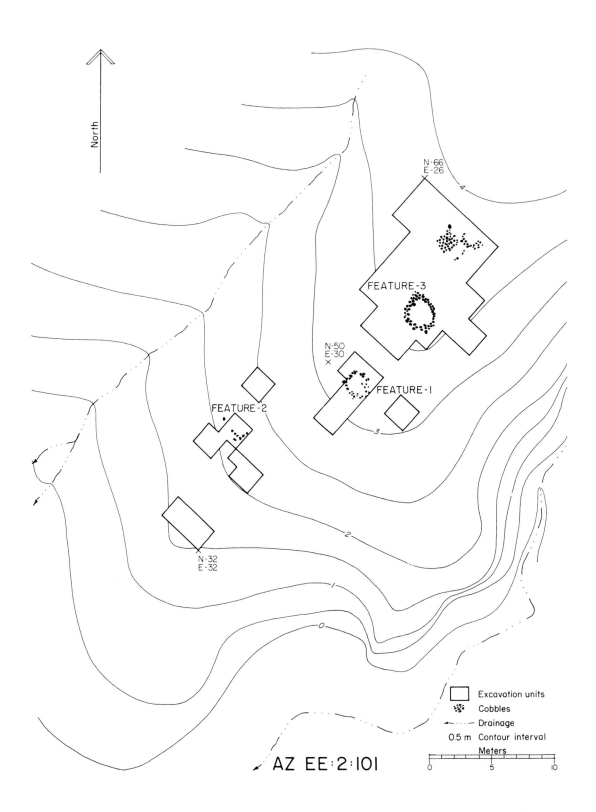

North

N-66
E-26

4

FEATURE-3

N-50
E-30
X

FEATURE-1

FEATURE-2

3

2

N-32
E-32

1

0

☐ Excavation units

🞄🞄 Cobbles

--·-- Drainage

0.5 m Contour interval

Meters

0   5   10

AZ EE:2:101

Figure 2.8 Map of AZ EE:2:101.

Feature 1

A somewhat circular cluster of angular quartzite cobbles on the surface approximately 2 m to 2.5 m in diameter was designated Feature 1 (Fig. 2.9). The cobbles range from 10 cm to 50 cm in maximum dimension with the larger cobbles restricted to the west half of the feature and the smaller ones more densely concentrated on the east half. Excavations revealed that the feature was sitting on a sterile surface, and had no depth. Associated artifacts consisted of a few flakes, and no artifacts were encountered during excavation. This feature may represent a house ring, the remnants of which consist of the rocks used to anchor the brush superstructure.

Feature 2

Feature 2 was an amorphous scatter of large, angular, quartzite cobbles in a 2-m-by-2-m area on the surface (Fig. 2.10). No order remained to the rocks, but their size and proximity to one another suggested that they may have been part of a feature of some type. A few artifacts were recovered during excavation of this area, but no further rocks were found. Feature 2 may also have served a function similar to that of Feature 1, but was later disturbed by cultural or natural processes.

Feature 3

A large, circular roasting pit (2.5 m by 3 m) containing a large quantity of fire-cracked rock was discovered near the east central part of the site (Figs. 2.11 and 2.12). The north half of the feature was excavated after definition, revealing a 40 cm deep pit with a shallow, basinlike cross section. Large rocks filled the entire pit, and it is estimated that over 200 were removed from the excavated portion of the feature. Charcoal, in the form of well-defined stick and branch segments as well as lumps, was abundant, and another unidentified carbonized substance, perhaps from the cooking of agave hearts, was found. A few pieces of flaked stone were the only artifacts recovered from the pit. Two radiocarbon dates on charcoal from the pit suggest it is an historic feature: 150 ± 90 B.P. (A-2932) and 140 ± 90 B.P. (A-2933).

Analysis of Artifacts

A total of 3193 artifacts and 85 pieces of unmodified bone were recovered from the excavations at AZ EE:2:100 and AZ EE:2:101 including surface and subsurface material. The analysis of this material was undertaken: (1) to help define and date the occupations of the sites and determine to what degree the sites were used through time; (2) to help interpret the kinds of activities that were occurring at the sites; and (3) to identify differences, if any, between the two sites.

Figure 2.9   Feature 1 at AZ EE:2:101 after excavation.

Figure 2.10   Feature 2 at AZ EE:2:101 after excavation.

Figure 2.11   Feature 3 at AZ EE:2:101 after exposure.

Figure 2.12   Feature 3 at AZ EE:2:101 after partial excavation.

Table 2.1 provides a tabulation of all the material recovered from Sycamore Canyon.

Table 2.1

COUNTS OF ARTIFACT CLASSES AND BONE RECOVERED FROM
THE SYCAMORE CANYON SITES

Artifact Class	AZ EE:2:100	AZ EE:2:101	Total
Flaked Stone	2529	370	2899
Ceramics	257	3	260
Ground Stone	33	1	34
Bone	85	0	85
Total	2904	374	3278

For the purposes of the analysis, the artifacts were divided into five categories: ceramics, flaked stone, ground stone, faunal material, and historic artifacts. Specialized analyses were carried out on the various samples collected including pollen and radiocarbon samples. An unknown carbonized substance recovered from both Feature 3 at AZ EE:2:100 and Feature 3 at AZ EE:2:101 was also analyzed to identify its makeup. Results of the analyses are presented in the following sections.

Flaked Stone

A total of 2899 pieces of flaked stone was recovered from the Sycamore Canyon sites, both from surface and subsurface contexts. The formal attributes of these artifacts reflect the cultural and temporal affinities of the sites, the preferred lithic material types used by the inhabitants, the types of stone working operations done at the site (such as raw material procurement, tool manufacture, and tool modification), and the tasks the tools were designed to perform. The flaked stone was further separated into two classes for analysis: lithic debris and retouched pieces. The assemblages from each site were evaluated on an individual basis, and then comparisons were made between them and to the assemblages from the Archaic and Hohokam flaked stone assemblages from the Rosemont area.

Debitage

Those flaked stone artifacts that consisted of unmodified complete and fragmentary flakes and shatter fragments were classified as debitage. These waste products were subjected to detailed study.

Methods of Study

The maximum size was recorded for each specimen with the size class table utilized by Huckell (1984: 96). Several other nonmetric variables were also recorded for each artifact: raw material type, the amount of cortex on the exterior surface of the flake, and the type of striking platform (cortical, plain, crushed, or faceted). These variables were recorded in an attempt to describe the types of reduction activities that were occurring at the sites.

Complete flakes are all flakes in which the striking platform, both lateral edges, and the distal edge are intact. Fragments with platforms are proximal flake fragments which retain all or most of the striking platform, but have lost, through breakage, the distal end of the flake. Fragments without platforms are distal and medial fragments which are missing, through breakage, the striking platform and portions of the lateral or distal ends. Split flakes are fragments that have been broken longitudinally from the point of percussion on the striking platform to the distal end of the piece, leaving a portion of the striking platform, one lateral edge, and a portion of the distal end intact. Shatter includes all irregular, angular pieces of debris in which the interior and exterior surfaces cannot be distinguished.

The maximum dimension of each piece of debitage was recorded using the metric size class chart, which is divided into arbitrarily numbered square units (Fig. 2.13). The amount of cortex on the exterior surface of the debitage was recorded on all pieces using three categories: 0-25 percent, 26-75 percent, and 76-100 percent. On those flakes or fragments with striking platforms, the platform type was recorded using four categories: cortical platforms (those entirely or partially covered with cortex); plain platforms (a plain, non-cortical surface with no flake scars); faceted platforms (those with portions of two or more flake scars running across their surface); and crushed platforms (those whose type cannot be determined since the platform was destroyed by crushing or shattering during removal of the flake).

Results

Table 2.2 presents the debitage divided by type for AZ EE:2:100 and AZ EE:2:101.

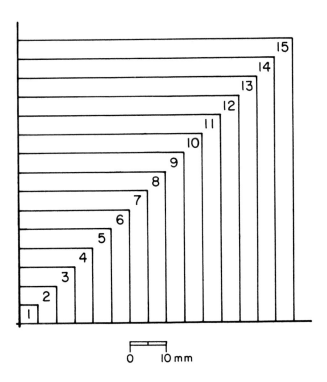

Figure 2.13 Size classes used in the analysis of the debitage from the
Sycamore Canyon sites.

        Both sites had much higher percentages of flake fragments than
complete flakes, with fragments more than twice as abundant. This is
similar to the assemblage of debitage from the Archaic sites from the
Rosemont area, except there were considerably fewer complete flakes from
the Rosemont sites (Fig. 2.14). The higher percentage of complete
flakes is most similar to the Hohokam site assemblages from the Rosemont
area, which have large numbers of complete flakes, approaching a 1:1
ratio to flake fragments. The size of the debitage varies significantly
between the two Sycamore Canyon sites. While the average flake size is
small in both samples, there are some noticeable differences as may be
seen from the flake size distribution presented in Figure 2.15. The
flake size curve from AZ EE:2:100 is highly peaked at Class 2, dropping
sharply to Class 5, which is very similar to the Rosemont Archaic
assemblage. By contrast, the curve from AZ EE:2:101 is a gentle arc
running from Class 2, gently peaking at class 4, and dropping slightly
to Class 7. This curve is similar to the Rosemont Hohokam assemblage
(Fig. 2.15).

        Fifteen raw material types were used by the inhabitants of the
Sycamore Canyon sites, but chert, quartzite, metasediment, and
silicified limestone were apparently the preferred materials in both
assemblages. These sites differ from the Rosemont sites, although some
similarities can be seen from the distributional graph presented in
Figure 2.16. The Hohokam utilized great quantities of quartzite and
metasediment and a slightly lesser amount of silicified limestone,
apparently preferring easily accessible local materials. These
materials, though medium- to coarse-grained, were suited to their
tool-making needs. The Archaic people preferred the finer grained,

Table 2.2

FLAKED STONE DEBITAGE AND CORES FROM
THE SYCAMORE CANYON SITES

Artifact Class	AZ EE:2:100	AZ EE:2:101	Total
Complete	827	105	932
Fragment with platform	375	48	423
Fragment without platform	994	113	1107
Split	70	8	78
Shatter	72	29	101
Retouched	180	59	239
Cores	11	8	19
Total	2529	370	2899

cryptocrystalline, siliceous materials for their tools, and used large quantities of chert brought in from other sources. They also made use of locally available metasediment and quartzite, but not in large quantities. The Sycamore Canyon assemblages resemble the Archaic assemblage from the Rosemont area, with the exception of the use of greater amounts of silicified limestone and an igneous material, but this may be a reflection of what materials were locally available.

Both sites were very similar in the quantity of cortex on debitage, with approximately 80 percent of the specimens having less than 25 percent cortex on them as may be seen in Figure 2.17. The Rosemont assemblages also follow this trend, although the Hohokam sites had more pieces of debitage with 25 to 75 percent cortex on them (Fig. 2.17). The assemblages are also alike in types of striking platforms, as shown in Figure 2.18, with more than 60 percent of the flakes having plain platforms, and less than 20 percent of each assemblage with cortical, faceted or crushed platforms. The Rosemont Hohokam assemblage is most similar to the Sycamore Canyon sites, while the Archaic assemblage has a lower percentage of plain platforms and a higher percentage of faceted platforms (Fig. 2.18).

Retouched Pieces

Retouched pieces were defined as pieces of flaked stone exhibiting evidence of secondary retouch with flakes removed from one or more edges, usually in a uniform fashion.

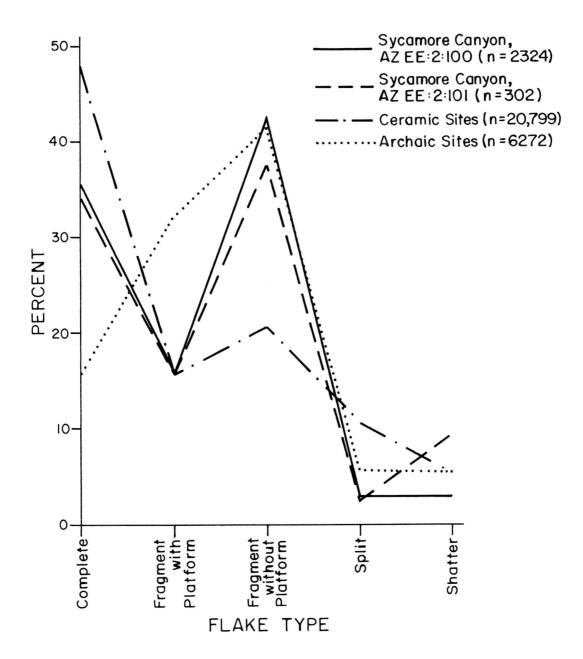

Figure 2.14 Frequencies of flaked stone debitage classes for the
Sycamore Canyon sites, Rosemont Archaic sites, and Rosemont Hohokam sites.

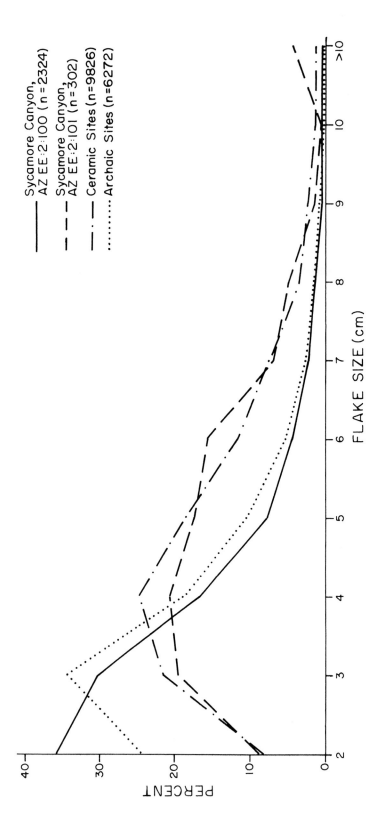

Figure 2.15 Debitage size distribution for the Sycamore Canyon sites, Rosemont Archaic sites, and Rosemont Hohokam sites.

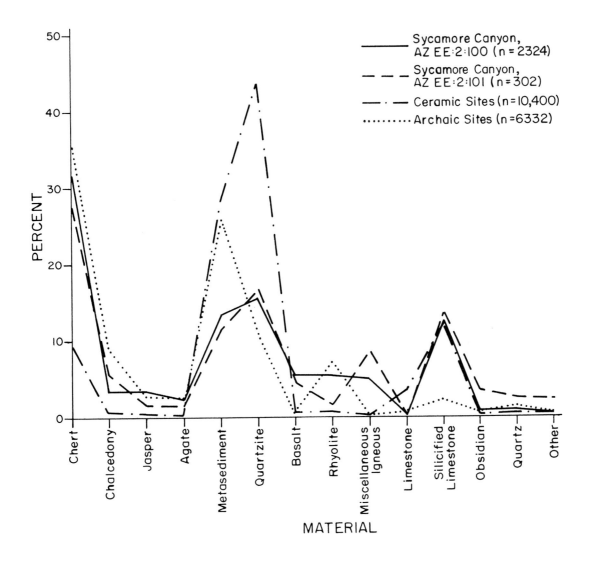

Figure 2.16 Raw material types for debitage from the Sycamore Canyon sites, Rosemont Archaic sites, and Rosemont Hohokam sites.

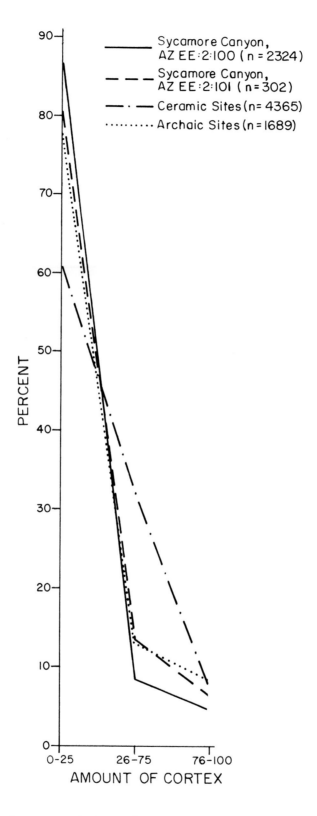

Figure 2.17 Relative quantities of cortex on debitage from the Sycamore Canyon sites, Rosemont Archaic sites, and Rosemont Hohokam sites.

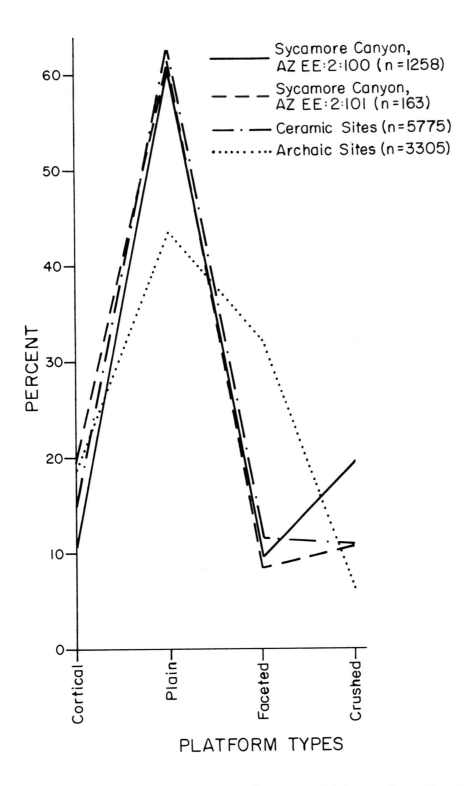

Figure 2.18 Types of striking platforms on debitage from the Sycamore Canyon sites, Rosemont Archaic sites, and Rosemont Hohokam sites.

Methods of Study

These artifacts were classified into one of eight artifact types based on morphology and similar to the traditionally defined tool types commonly employed in the Southwest. The type names do not necessarily suggest function, since use-wear was not always present to indicate how, or in some cases if, the pieces had been utilized as tools. These pieces were further divided within the artifact categories to distinguish variations within the specific artifact types. Finally, a number of metric and nonmetric attributes were recorded on each retouched piece, including material type, completeness, and presence or absence of edge damage. A total of 239 retouched pieces was recovered, 180 from AZ EE:2:100 (7.1 percent of the lithic assemblage from that site) and 59 from AZ EE:2:101 (15.9 percent of the sample) (Table 2.3). The eight artifact types are defined in the following paragraphs.

Scrapers are unifacially retouched pieces which have a series of flakes removed from a flat surface, usually the interior of a flake, along one or more margins to create a fairly steep working edge. Because of the variability among scrapers, four different subtypes were used, depending on the artifact size and type of edge retouch. First are large, irregularly retouched scrapers, which are heavy, thick pieces exhibiting slightly uneven retouch on one or two edges, usually made on chunks or cores exceeding 60 mm in maximum dimension. They are generally believed to be associated with the Hohokam. Second, there are small, regularly retouched scrapers, generally made on small chunks or flakes less than 50 mm in maximum dimension, and exhibiting a fine, even retouch on one or two edges. This scraper type is more commonly associated with Archaic sites. Third are ovoid scrapers, those pieces, small or large, with retouch along their entire margin, and due to their convex side are occasionally called "turtle-back" scrapers. Finally, there are denticulate scrapers which exhibit a series of widely spaced flake scars creating a sawlike, serrated edge. Fragments too small to accurately place in the above categories were typed as indeterminate.

Unifaces constitute a broad category that includes all pieces exhibiting unifacial retouch, but which are generally smaller, thinner, and exhibit more variability and less uniformity in edge shape than scrapers. Due to the variation in retouch, five subtypes were used, as well as a fragment category to cover those pieces to incomplete for identification. First are single-edged unifaces which have relatively uniform retouch on one edge. Second, there are double-edged unifaces with relatively uniform retouch on two edges. Third, are unpatterned retouched pieces with a small number of nonoverlapping flake scars on one or more surfaces. The fourth category includes fine flake tools, which are small flakes exhibiting one or more working edges produced by uniformly overlapping tiny flakes. Finally, there are spokeshaves, which exhibit a concavity on one edge produced by the removal of two or more flakes in a uniform fashion.

Perforators are defined as retouched pieces exhibiting a projection produced by unifacial or bifacial retouch. Two subtypes were recognized based on the size of the projection: gravers and drills.

TABLE 2.3

SUMMARY OF RETOUCHED PIECES AND CORES
BY TYPE FOR THE SYCAMORE CANYON SITES

Artifact Type	AZ EE:2:100	AZ EE:2:101	Total
Scrapers	21 (11.7)	14 (23.7)	35
Large	7	7	14
Small	8	5	13
Ovoid	1	0	1
Denticulate	3	1	4
Unidentified	2	1	3
Unifaces	46 (25.6)	16 (27.1)	62
Single	7	2	9
Double	1	0	1
Spokeshave	4	0	4
Unpatterned	7	5	12
Fine flake	4	5	9
Unidentified	23	3	26
Perforators	10 (5.6)	1 (1.7)	11
Graver	3	0	3
Drill	1	0	1
Graver fragment	1	0	1
Drill fragment	2	1	3
Drill-scraper	1	0	1
Graver-scraper	1	0	1
Bifaces	51 (28.3)	10 (17.0)	61
Biface	4	1	5
Preform	10	2	12
Biface end fragment	17	3	20
Preform end fragment	11	2	13
Biface midsection	3	0	3
Preform midsection	0	1	1
Wedge	3	1	4
Unidentified	3	0	3

( ) = Percent of site assemblage

83

SUMMARY OF RETOUCHED PIECES AND CORES
BY TYPE FOR THE SYCAMORE CANYON SITES

Artifact Type	AZ EE:2:100	AZ EE:2:101	Total
Projectile Points	44 (24.4)	4 (6.8)	48
Tapering stemmed	3	0	3
Pinto style	4	0	4
Large triangular	15	3	18
Corner notched	4	0	4
Side & basal notched	3	0	3
Rillito style	3	0	3
Small triangular	1	0	1
Untypable	3	0	3
Tip or medial fragment	4	0	4
Basal fragment	4	1	5
Cobble Tools	5 (2.8)	12 (20.3)	17
Cobble hammerstone	3	5	8
Cobble chopper	2	4	6
Core hammerstone	0	3	3
Knives	3 (1.7)	2 (3.4)	5
Large flake	2	0	2
Tabular	1	2	3
Total Retouched Pieces	180	59	239
Cores	11 (0.4)	8 (2.2)	19
Single	0	1	1
Double	5	2	7
Multiple	6	3	9
Globular	0	2	2
Total Artifacts	191	67	258

( ) = Percent of site assemblage

Gravers have small projections which have been produced with minimal work, many being created with the removal of two flakes to isolate a tip. Drills have long projections or "bits" made with extensive, usually bifacial, retouching. Several perforators were made on scrapers, and fragments of perforators were classified separately.

Bifaces are those pieces exhibiting bifacial flake removal from a common, continuous margin. Three separate types of bifacially worked implements were recognized: bifaces, preforms, and wedges. Bifaces represent what were considered to be finished tools, thin implements exhibiting even, overlapping flake scars and displaying a lanceolate shape. Preforms appear more crudely flaked, being larger and thicker than bifaces. With their large, unevenly spaced flake scars and irregular shape, they probably represent unfinished bifaces. Wedges are flakes or chunks which have been used to split objects such as bone or wood. They are characterized by opposed, crushed margins from which sheer fracture scars, with flat percussion features, originate. The retouch is not intentional, but a result of the use of the object.

Projectile Points are small bifaces (20 mm to 60 mm long), usually triangular or lanceolate in shape, that have some specialization in form, such as stems or notches, to facilitate hafting.

Cobble tools are natural river cobbles with one or more edges modified by intentional retouch or through use. Three subtypes were defined based on the type of retouch or use-wear. Cobble hammerstones, the first type, exhibit battered margins from use as hammers to remove flakes from cores, or from use in other battering tasks. The second type, cobble choppers, have one edge modified by the removal of flakes to produce an edge for cutting. Core hammerstones, the third type, are pieces which have had two or more flakes removed from a margin and exhibit battering over the flaked margins from use as hammers.

Knives are large flakes or tabular pieces of lithic material which have one or more (usually one) unifacially or bifacially flaked edges with regularly spaced, overlapping flake scars to create a working edge. They usually fit in the hand comfortably and are commonly called mescal or tabular knives.

Cores are defined as pieces of lithic material which have had large flakes removed from them and exhibit negative bulbs of percussion. They were divided into four subtypes depending on the number of striking platforms used to remove flakes: single, double, and multiple platform, and a fourth category for nonglobular pieces with two or more large flakes removed to test the material. Material type, amount of cortex, and weight were the three attributes recorded on cores.

Results

Scrapers were recovered from both sites, with 21 (11.7 percent of retouched pieces) from AZ EE:2:100 and 14 (23.7 percent) from AZ EE:2:101. These percentages are similar to that from the Archaic sites (Fig. 2.19). Large and small scrapers were found in approximately

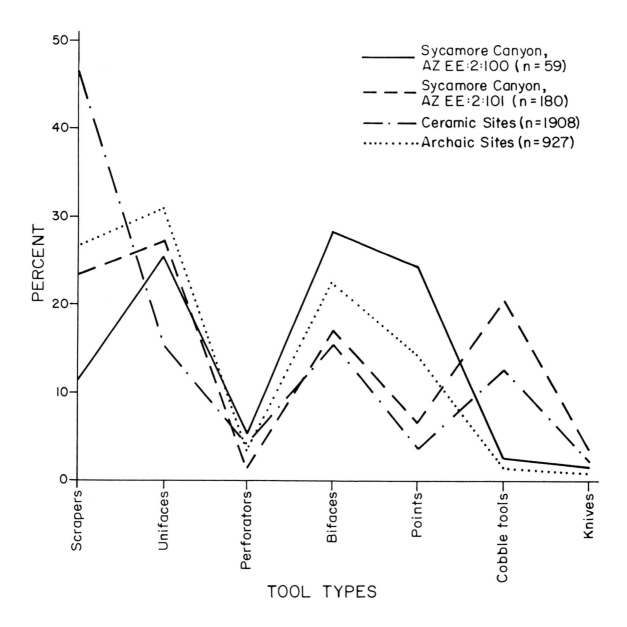

Figure 2.19 Frequencies of retouched tools from the Sycamore Canyon sites, Rosemont Archaic sites, and Rosemont Hohokam sites.

equal numbers, although AZ EE:2:100 had a higher percentage of small scrapers, and a high percentage of large scrapers was seen at AZ EE:2:101. Ovoid and denticulate scrapers were seen in small numbers from both sites. Coarser-grained materials such as quartzite and metasediment were most commonly used for scrapers.

Unifaces make up over 25 percent of the retouched pieces from both sites with 46 (25.6 percent) from AZ EE:2:100 and 16 (27.1 percent) from AZ EE:2:101, which is similar to the Archaic assemblage (Fig. 2.19). Of these, nearly half are unidentifiable fragments which probably represent pieces from a variety of tool types. Chert and other fine-grained material was commonly used for unifaces.

Perforators were recovered in small numbers from both Sycamore Canyon sites and the Hohokam and Archaic sites from Rosemont (Fig. 2.19). AZ EE:2:100 had the largest number with 10 (55.6 percent) while AZ EE:2:101 only had one (1.7 percent). Chert and rhyolite were preferred materials for these implements.

Bifaces were found ranging in size from 42 mm to 52 mm long, 18 mm to 31 mm wide, and 6 mm to 8 mm thick. Chert and other fine-grained materials were preferred for biface manufacture, although more coarse-grained material, especially silicified limestone, was also used. Bifaces and preforms occur in equal numbers, and approximately 70 percent of the implements are fragmentary. AZ EE:2:100 has a large number of bifaces (51, or 28.3 percent), and they are the most numerous artifact from that site. This is very similar to the Archaic sites in the Rosemont area which, as a rule, have larger numbers of bifaces. The lower number of bifaces seen at AZ EE:2:100 is most similar to the Hohokam assemblage (Fig. 2.19) in the Rosemont area.

The projectile points from AZ EE:2:100 are the best evidence of the long occupational history of this locus. Six separate styles of points may be identified that range in age from Middle Archaic to Protohistoric. In the following paragraphs each of these styles is described and discussed, and a representative selection of typical specimens is presented in Figure 2.20.

By far the most abundant style is a simple, large, triangular point with a concave base. Fifteen examples of this form were recovered, and although these vary in length and to some extent in configuration, all clearly represent the same style. Figure 2.20g-k may convey some feeling for this variability. There are, in addition, two other specimens that display very wide, shallow-sided notches (Fig. 2.201); these are felt to be a variant of the triangular concave base style.

Though dependant to some extent on the amount of reworking a particular specimen has undergone, it appears that this point style was produced largely by percussion technique, followed by selective pressure flaking to produce the basal concavity, even the margins, and sharpen the tip. Reworked examples (Fig. 2.20k) may display only pressure flake scars. A variety of fine- to medium-grained raw materials is represented, including chert and chalcedony (6), metamorphosed sediment (7), and indurated limestone (2).

Figure 2.20 Projectile points from AZ EE:2:100 (a-l, o-q) and
AZ EE:2:101 (m-n). a, Protohistoric point; b, Hohokam point; c-d,
unknown point style; e-f, probable San Pedro points; g-n, Archaic
triangular concave base points; n-o, Pinto points; q, Archaic
tapering stemmed point.

Though it appears to occur widely throughout the southern part of Arizona and is certainly preceramic, this point style remains poorly dated and of unknown diagnostic value. Three points of this style were recovered from a site along Davidson Canyon during the ANAMAX-Rosemont Project testing phase in 1979 (Huckell 1980: 170-172), and it was suggested at that time that the style might be of Late Archaic age based on its association with typical San Pedro points at a site near Fairbank in the San Pedro Valley (see Cattanach 1966). Since that time I have been shown numerous triangular concave base points by Lisa Huckell, who recovered them from a mixed site at the mouth of Pima Canyon north of Tucson, and by Jon Czaplicki, whose Tucson Aqueduct survey crews found such points at sites scattered from east of Picacho to the Avra Valley west of Tucson. In addition, Simpson and Wells (1983: Fig. 23) recovered this style from the surfaces of ten sites in Saguaro National Monument, Rincon Mountain Unit. Of interest is the fact that four of these sites also yielded San Pedro points, adding an admittedly minor amount of evidence that the style may, in fact, be Late Archaic. Finally, examination of the projectile points from several of Whalen's sites on the eastern flanks of the Whetstone Mountains revealed that one (AZ EE:3:8) produced a number of triangular concave base points. Whalen (1971: 189) apparently considered the site to be of Chiricahua stage (Middle Archaic) age. It is felt that this is less likely, based on the absence of this style at undoubted Middle Archaic sites such as Lone Hill (Agenbroad 1970), but until recovered from contexts associated with materials suitable for radiocarbon dating, the exact temporal range of the triangular concave base style will remain unknown. So, too, its utility as a cultural marker must await future evaluation from other sites.

Following the triangular concave base points in abundance were two other Archaic projectile point styles, each of which is represented by four specimens. First of these is the Pinto point style (Amsden 1935; Harrington 1957). All four are of the same basic style as the two illustrated specimens (Fig. 2.20o and p), and would fall within the range of Harrington's Sloping Shoulders Subtype (Harrington 1957: 51). One is made of chalcedony, one of metamorphosed sediment, and two are of very fine-grained rhyolite (rhyolitic jasper). Abundantly distributed throughout southern Arizona and the greater Southwest (Huckell 1984), these points are evidence of Middle Archaic occupation of Sycamore Canyon.

Also represented by four specimens is a corner-notched style of dart point indicative of Late Archaic use of the site. The two more complete specimens (Fig. 2.20e and f), both of chert, appear to be rather small examples of San Pedro style points, though it is also possible that they represent an as-yet-unnamed, corner-notched point style probably of slightly younger age (see Huckell 1984: 165). Of the remaining two specimens, one is a basal fragment that clearly represents the unnamed corner notched style and the other is a blade fragment too small to classify beyond "corner-notched". The latter two are both of metamorphosed sediment.

Three other projectile point styles are represented by three specimens each. The first of these is a tapering stemmed form described from four sites in the Rosemont area (Huckell 1984); the most complete example from AZ EE:2:100 is illustrated in Figure 2.20q. Two of the specimens are made of metamorphosed sediment and the third is of rhyolite. One of them displays more recent flake scars around its margins that cut a patinated surface--it is tentatively classified as a tapering stemmed form, based on the assumption that the reworking mimicked, rather than changed, the original form of the specimen. This style too is poorly dated, but has been suggested to be of Early Archaic age.

Another style represented by three relatively small side- and basal-notched points was identified. The two complete chert specimens are illustrated in Figure 2.20c and d; the third example, of obsidian, is a longitudinally split fragment. Neither the age nor the cultural affiliation of these specimens is clear. Conceivably they could be either small dart points or arrow points, and are not immediately diagnostic of either the Archaic or Hohokam components at AZ EE:2:100.

Clearly representing the Hohokam occupation of the site are three complete arrow points of chert (2) and chalcedony (1). Each has a short, rather broad blade (crudely serrated on two) a very small, short contracting stem (Fig. 2.20b). Kelly (1978, Fig. 6.7) has suggested that this form is typical of the Rillito phase; work at the Hohokam sites in the Rosemont area (Rozen 1984) indicates a predominantly Colonial temporal range.

Finally, a very small, triangular, chert arrow point with a deeply concave base and shallow side-notches was recovered from AZ EE:2:100 (Fig. 2.20a). This style is typical of the points found at Sobaipuri or Upper Pima sites in southern Arizona (see Doyel 1977, Fig. 73, Rows a-c), and thus suggests a Protohistoric or early Historic component at the site.

An additional 11 specimens were recovered that were untypable because their shapes were too amorphous from damage or reworking, or because they were too fragmentary. Three examples fell into the first category, and the remaining eight were in the second.

Of the more amorphous, untypable specimens, two were very roughly diamond- or lozenge-shaped in outline. One of these was a small, very crudely flaked piece of agate, while the second, larger one was made of dark chert and exhibited relatively well-controlled flaking. This second point nonetheless was rather irregular in outline from damage; it could originally have been either diamond-shaped or foliate in appearance. The third amorphous point, also of dark chert, was roughly triangular in shape, and similar in size to the contracting stem arrow points described above. However, the base of this specimen was very irregular in outline, suggesting the possibility that it had never been finished.

The remaining eight specimens include three tip fragments, two of which are from rhyolite dart points and one chalcedony example that could represent either a dart or an arrow point. A small chalcedony basal fragment also falls in this same equivocal size range, but two other basal fragments of obsidian and jasper represent some type of arrow point. Rounding out this group is a large, serrated midsection of a rhyolite arrow or dart point and a small fragment of metamorphosed sediment that may represent either the tip or basal corner of a dart point.

AZ EE:2:101 yielded four projectile points, three of which are sufficiently complete to be typed and one which is a midsection. The three more complete specimens are representatives of the same triangular concave base dart point style so abundant at AZ EE:2:100. Two of these appear in Figure 2.20m and n. The larger specimen is made of rhyolite and exhibits well-controlled flaking; it is easily the best made point of this style that was recovered from either site. The smaller point is made of metamorphosed sediment, and has been heavily reworked. It is similar in size to the third specimen from the site, a white chert point that was also reworked after impact damage.

The midsection fragment is of yellow jasper but is too fragmentary to suggest anything of its original form.

The relative amounts of cobble tools differed greatly between the two sites, with 12 (20.3 percent of the site sample) from AZ EE:2:101, and only 5 (2.8 percent) from AZ EE:2:100. The high percentage from AZ EE:2:101 is very similar to the large numbers of cobble tools recovered from Hohokam sites in the Rosemont area, and the low number found at AZ EE:2:100 more closely resembles the low quantities found on Archaic sites (Fig. 2.19). Quartzite river cobbles are the most common lithic material used for cobble tools, although other coarse-grained materials were also utilized.

Knives represent a small percentage of the retouched pieces from both sites, with three (1.7 percent) from AZ EE:2:100 and two (3.4 percent) from AZ EE:2:101, and are not common in either the Hohokam or Archaic assemblages from Rosemont (Fig. 2.19). Medium- to coarse-grained materials were used as a rule, with an unknown igneous material being the most common. Materials of tabular form or fracture were used as well. Approximately equal numbers of both the large flake and tabular forms were recovered.

Only small numbers of cores were recovered, 11 (0.4 percent of the assemblage) from AZ EE:2:100 and 8 (2.2 percent of the assemblage) from AZ EE:2:101. The majority (50 percent) have less than 25 percent cortex remaining on them, and double and multiple platform cores are the most common types (80 percent). The cores tend to be small, exhausted or nearly exhausted, ranging from 39 mm to 86 mm in length, 34 mm to 77 mm in width, and 16 mm to 55 mm in thickness. They weigh from 46 g to 197 g, except for one large specimen at 330 g. Metasediment was the most common material (50 percent), and with the exception of two chert cores, the remainder are of coarse-grained material.

One other artifact from AZ EE:2:100 should also be mentioned. A large quartz crystal fragment, with a maximum dimension of 2.5 cm, was found on the surface of the site. While it is unworked, it was clearly imported to the site, possibly for ritual use.

Discussion

The flaked stone assemblages from AZ EE:2:100 and AZ EE:2:101 are characterized by a high percentage of broken flakes (59.7 percent and 53.5 percent respectively), and low percentages of retouched pieces (7.1 percent and 15.9 percent respectively) and cores (0.4 percent and 2.2 percent respectively). The flakes tend to be small and are generally produced from locally available, coarse-grained materials, although a high percentage of fine-grained chert was also used. Cortex on the debitage is generally lacking, with most flakes having no cortex at all. These characteristics suggest that secondary reduction (including tool production or resharpening) was the principle task occurring at the Sycamore Canyon sites. Secondary reduction is characterized by a high frequency of flake fragments, by low frequencies of whole flakes, cores, retouched pieces and hammerstones, and by small flakes with very little cortex (Rozen 1981: 206).

While there are many similarities in the collections from the two sites, there are many noticeable differences that may reflect differing temporal and cultural attributes of the sites. The lithic analyses of the Hohokam and Archaic sites in the Rosemont area (Rozen 1984; Huckell 1984) have provided comparative material to aid in the interpretation of the Sycamore Canyon sites. Archaic sites are characterized by well-made tools, large numbers of unifaces and finely-flaked scrapers, and points and bifaces. The debitage consists of small, noncortical flakes with a heavy reliance on fine-grained, cryptocrystalline lithic materials such as chert and chalcedony (Huckell 1984). The Hohokam assemblage is characterized by large numbers of heavy scrapers and cobble tools, crudely made and bulky, and few bifaces and projectile points. The debitage is characterized by medium and large flakes of locally available, coarse-grained lithic materials such as quartzite, metasediment, and silicified limestone. Complete flakes and flake fragments are approximately equal in number, and high percentages of plain platforms and noncortical flakes may be observed (Rozen 1984).

Comparisons of the assemblages from the Sycamore Canyon sites with those from Rosemont revealed that the AZ EE:2:100 assemblage was most similar to the Archaic sites assemblage, while the AZ EE:2:101 assemblage was more like the Hohokam sites collection. At AZ EE:2:100 this is especially noticeable in the occurrence of larger numbers of finely worked retouched pieces (including small bifaces and projectile points of Archaic styles), the high percentage of small flakes (peaking at 3 cm), and the utilization of fine-grained material. On the other hand, AZ EE:2:101 has a rather low number of bifaces and projectile points, but a greater number of large, poorly made scrapers and other crudely made, bulky tools. Also high percentages of medium (3 cm to 6 cm) and large (7 cm to 9 cm) flakes were present at these sites. The two Sycamore Canyon sites are also similar in many ways: the complete-flake-to-fragment ratios (Table 2.2); use of similar lithic materials probably locally available in Sycamore Canyon; a general lack of cortex on flakes; and the relative percentages of certain retouched pieces such as perforators and knives.

The projectile points represent the only temporally and culturally diagnostic markers in the lithic assemblage, although many of them can only be roughly placed. They do reveal a long utilization of the sites, ranging from the Early or Middle Archaic through the Protohistoric or Historic Sobaipuri.

Ceramics

A total of 260 sherds was recovered from the Sycamore Canyon sites, 257 from AZ EE:2:100 and three from AZ EE:2:101, indicating that the Hohokam had utilized both sites. All but two of the sherds were common Tucson Basin types, with two intrusives from the Salt-Gila Basin area recovered from AZ EE:2:100.

Plain Ware

Undecorated, unslipped plain ware made up the majority of the ceramics from both sites (89 percent or 231 sherds), as is common for Hohokam sites. Four types of plain ware were identified, based on the composition of the temper and the finish of the surface, as defined by Deaver (1984).

Type 1 is a nonmicaceous brown ware with coarse to medium sand temper. It is crudely made by coiling, and finger imprints are commonly visible. This type is predominantly small or miniature vessels, and is similar to Alma Plain.

Type 2 is a paddle-and-anvil-constructed, lightly micaceous brown ware with a sand temper and smoothed surface. The mica occurs as individual platelets and is interpreted to be inclusions in the wash sand used for temper. Type 2 plain ware is the dominant pottery type in all Hohokam phases except Rillito, and is seen at Classic period sites in the Tucson Basin as well.

Type 3 is a paddle-and-anvil-constructed, heavily micaceous, brown ware tempered with medium-grained sand and crushed mica schist. It differs from Type 2 in that the mica covers virtually all of the surface of this type, causing a shiny effect, although a small amount of overlap does occur between the two types. Type 3 is indistinguishable from Gila Plain. Type 3 plain ware reached its greatest frequency during the Rillito phase.

Type 4 is distinguished by the use of crushed phyllite or other micaceous rock in the temper, and differs from Type 3 because only large plates of phyllite appear without the small, crushed pieces. It is generally considered similar to Wingfield Plain. Temporally, it is similar to Type 3, reaching its peak during the Rillito phase.

None of the plain wares are good temporal markers, ranging as they do from the early Colonial through the late Sedentary periods of Tucson Basin prehistory, although Type 2 is more common in the Sedentary period, and Type 3 is less common at that time. All four types are present through the entire Hohokam occupation of the Rosemont area. Seventeen sherds from AZ EE:2:100 (7.4 percent of the plain ware from that site) were two eroded to be placed in any category and were left unclassified.

Two Type 1 sherds were recovered, both from AZ EE:2:100, including the rim of a small bowl and a possible scoop fragment, both common vessel forms for this type.

Type 2 plain ware is the most common type of plain ware, making up 54.2 percent (124 sherds) of the plain ware from AZ EE:2:100 and 66.6 percent (2 sherds) from AZ EE:2:101. Only two vessel rims were recovered, both from bowls.

Type 3 sherds were found only at AZ EE:2:100, making up 37.1 percent of the sample. Five rims were recovered, all from jars, which is unusual since bowls were the most common vessel form in the Rosemont collection (Deaver 1984).

Only one Type 4 sherd was recovered from AZ EE:2:100, comprising 0.4 percent of the sample.

Decorated Ware

Decorated ware was recovered only from AZ EE:2:100, comprising 10.8 percent (28 sherds) of that sample. Of those sherds recovered, less than half could be identified as to type due to their small size and poor condition: 2 (7.1 percent) were identified only as decorated, and 13 (46.4 percent) were identified only as red-on-brown sherds. The type descriptions from Deaver (1984) were used to aid in the classification of the remaining 13 sherds.

Rillito Red-on-brown represents the hallmark of the Colonial style (A.D. 700-900) with maximum control of the firing atmosphere reached in order to obtain a light colored background ranging from light brown, to tan, to dark gray. The paste is generally fine-grained and there is a preference for crushed schist as the main tempering material, although there is an increase in the percentage of sand temper from the preceding Canada del Oro phase (A.D. 500-700). Decoratively, Rillito Red-on-brown is unsurpassed in the intricacy and draftsmanship of the design, with a very fine control of line work and an overall smallness about the decoration. The most common feature is the use of one or two decorative units, repeated to create a complex design. Many Rillito decorations present the optical illusion of motion. Exterior trailing lines are common, usually consisting of four opposing lines. Most sherds exhibit a light to moderate polish. Four Rillito Red-on-brown sherds were recovered from AZ EE:2:100, ranging from Level 1 (0 to 10 cmbs) to Level 5 (40 to 50 cmbs). Three of the sherds are tan, with exterior decoration, and one is gray with an interior decoration. All are lightly polished on the decorated surface. Very little decoration remains due to the small size of the sherds.

Rincon Red-on-brown spans the Sedentary period (A.D. 900-1200), representing a continuation of Rillito Red-on-brown, but differing in aspects of decoration and technology. Surface color ranges from orangish brown, to brown, to dark gray, and surfaces are usually fire clouded, indicating a decline in control of the firing atmosphere. Smudging of bowl interiors also becomes common. Rincon Red-on-brown differs from Rillito Red-on-brown in that sand is the dominant temper type. By the middle of the Sedentary Period, schist is not used at all, and Rincon Red-on-brown can be recognized by its lack of mica. Three different varieties are recognized within this type. Style A is a continuation of the Colonial style with banded design layouts, but brushwork is heavier and much less precise than the earlier Rillito Red-on-brown. Schist is still used with sand in the temper, but it is no longer proportionately dominant. This style spans the entire Rincon Phase (Deaver 1984).

Style B emphasizes a highly gridlike pattern using smaller geometric spaces, and either rectangles, diamonds, or triangles to subdivide the decorative field instead of the banded designs used up to this point. Instead of the repetition of one or two decorative units, large numbers of units are used in a single design. This becomes the hallmark of the middle Sedentary period. Rim lips are always painted in this period also. There is also a refinement in the brushwork, and improvement in the draftsmanship, and the shift to all sand temper becomes complete. This style was present in the middle Rincon phase, approximately A.D. 1000-1100 (Deaver 1984).

Style C is similar to Style B in decorative structure, although there is a greater use of open space and a simplification of the design. This style is equivalent to what has been called Cortaro Red-on-brown and is intermediate between Style B and the Classic period (A.D. 1100-1200).

One Rincon Red-on-brown Style A sherd is in the sample from AZ EE:2:100, with minimal schist in the temper and exhibiting a curvilinear exterior design on a buff-colored background. Three sherds of Style B were recovered, a jar and two bowl fragments, including two rim sherds. Designs are common Rincon motifs including interlocking curvilinear scrolls, parallel wavy and straight lines, and hachure-filled bands. All three sherds are also fire-clouded black on the decorated surfaces, and the two rims are painted. One sherd from AZ EE:2:100 was placed in Style C; it displays an exterior decoration on a fire-clouded surface, exhibiting parallel lines, one of which is fringed.

Two sherds, including one rim sherd, could only be classified as Rincon Red-on-brown, style unknown, due to their small size and, therefore, limited design attributes.

Two intrusive sherds of Santa Cruz Red-on-buff, from the Salt-Gila area, were recovered from AZ EE:2:100. This type is diagnostic for the Santa Cruz phase of the Colonial period, dating to approximately A.D. 700-900. Santa Cruz Red-on-buff has a buff slip tending towards a pinkish hue, good quality brushwork with thin lines, scanty use of solid

elements and tight packing of motifs. Typical designs include the use
of nested chevrons and scroll motifs, and life forms are not uncommon
(Haury 1976: 210-212). Both sherds have buff slips on the decorated
surface, and have rectilinear designs. The type is contemporaneous with
Rillito Red-on-brown in the Tucson Basin.

Red Ware

One red ware sherd was found at AZ EE:2:101 that fits the
description of Rincon Red as defined by Greenleaf (1975: 59). Rincon
Red is characterized by a coarse, granular, sand-tempered paste that is
generally nonmicaceous. Vessels may be highly polished on either or
both surfaces. The slip is deep red, but weathering causes it to become
powdery and fugitive, and it may pit or flake. The exteriors vary from
tan to red due to firing. The recovered sherd is exterior slipped and
heavily weathered and pitted. Rincon Red is contemporaneous with Rincon
Red-on-brown and dates to the A.D. 900-1200 period.

Worked Sherds

Two sherds that had been ground to shape were found at
AZ EE:2:100, one in Feature 1 and one in Feature 3. Both are plain
ware, one Type 2 and one Type 3, and the fragments indicate that they
were either round or oval in shape when they were whole. Sherds such as
these, without perforations, are commonly called gaming pieces.

Discussion

All the pottery found at the Sycamore Canyon sites, with the
exception of two sherds, represents common Tucson Basin types. The two
intrusive sherds, both Santa Cruz Red-on-buff, indicate that there was
contact between the Hohokam in this area and those in the Salt-Gila
Basin during the Rillito phase (A.D. 700-900).

The ceramic assemblage is characterized by a high percentage of
temporally inspecific plain ware and a small number of decorated sherds
which can be dated more precisely. The occurrence of Rillito and Rincon
Red-on-brown sherds, as well as the occurrence of the Santa Cruz Red-on-
buff sherds, suggest that AZ EE:2:100 was utilized by the Hohokam
between A.D. 700-1200. Table 2.4 provides a tabulation of the sherds by
unit and level AZ EE:2:100. The recovery of sherds almost exclusively
from the eastern half of AZ EE:2:100 (east of E62), as well as sherds
from all three features on the site, would indicate that this portion of
the site was most heavily utilized by the Hohokam. The only sherds
found west of E62 were just below the surface in Level 1 and were
probably secondarily deposited there. The mixture of Archaic projectile
points with the ceramic period artifacts also indicates that the Hohokam
occupation disturbed an earlier Archaic deposit on the site, which
originally probably covered the entire site area.

TABLE 2.4

SHERD COUNTS BY UNIT AND
LEVEL FOR AZ EE:2:100

		Excavated Levels[1]					
Unit	Surface	1	2	3	4	5	6
N14E20							
N14E28							
N18E30							
N12E36		1					
N18E36							
N22E38		1					
N12E44							
N18E46		1					
N20E50							
N12E52							
N20E52							
N16E54							
N12E60							
N14E62		1					
N16E62			4				
N20E62	1	1	3				
N22E62	2	2					
N18E66	1	2	3	3	1		
N18E68	1	1	8	4	4	4	1
N18E70	1	7					
N24E72	1	36	8	1	4		
N16E90		8	18	8	9		
N18E90		2	8				
Feature 1	4	76	2	1	1	3	
Feature 2			5				
Feature 3[1]	—	2[2]	2[3]	—	—	—	—
Total	11	136	59	17	19	7	1

[1]With the exception of Feature 3, all excavations used arbitrary 10-cm levels.

[2]Combined levels 1 and 2.

[3]Combined levels 3 and 4.

The sherds at AZ EE:2:100 were found as deep as Level 6
(50 to 60 cmbs), with the bulk of ceramics found in Levels 1 and 2.
This suggests a relatively long utilization of this portion of the site,
which is supported by the number of Hohokam artifacts recovered. It is
probable that AZ EE:2:101 was occupied during this same period, although
only the possible Rincon Red sherd gives any indication of a date,
A.D. 900-1200. The few sherds recovered at this site and their lack of
depth suggests light Hohokam use of the area. The dates from the
ceramics at the two Sycamore Canyon sites correspond with the major
occupation of the Rosemont area to the south, and it is possible that
these sites were utilized by the same general group of people.

Ground Stone

The analysis of the ground stone artifacts was handled similarly
to the analysis of the flaked stone, with a number of attributes being
recorded for each piece. These included artifact type, material type,
completeness, and maximum length, width, and thickness. A total of 34
ground stone artifacts was recovered, 33 from AZ EE:2:100, and 1 from
AZ EE:2:101, including 24 manos, 8 metates, 1 pecked stone, and an
unidentified ground stone fragment (Table 2.5). These artifacts were
used to process nonagricultural and possibly agricultural plant foods.
Locally available material was used for their manufacture, dominated by
an unidentified igneous material (17 specimens, or 50 percent) and
quartzite (9 specimens, or 26 percent), with a few examples of vesicular
basalt, rhyolitic porphyry, gabbro, and sandstone.

Table 2.5

TABULATION OF GROUND STONE ARTIFACTS AT AZ EE:2:100

Artifact Class	Grid Squares	Feature 1	TOTAL
Metates:			
trough		1	1(3%)
basin	1	2	3(9.1%)
flat	1	2	3(9.1%)
indeterminate	3		3(9.1%)
Manos:			
handstone	4	1	5(15.2%)
mano	1	1	2(6.1%)
handstone-mano fragments	15		15(45.5%)
Pecked stone	1		1(3%)
Indeterminate form	1		1(3%)

Manos

Twenty-three manos, or mano fragments, were identified in the analysis, including the one piece of ground stone from AZ EE:2:101. Manos are the hand-held grinding implement used by both preceramic and ceramic cultural groups throughout the Southwest and are typically subdivided into manos and handstones on the basis of size and shape.

Manos generally include the two-handed or trough mano, usually pecked to shape over the entire surface, and loaf-shaped or rectilinear with length greater than width for use in a trough metate. They are associated with the Hohokam, and were present throughout their occupation of the Rosemont area, approximately A.D. 700-1100 (Tagg 1984). Only two manos were identified, both from AZ EE:2:100. One was a complete quartzite specimen, irregularly shaped, with trough end wear on its one undamaged end. Its dimensions are 14.2 cm long by 9.2 cm wide by 4.2 cm thick, falling well within the range of manos from the Ceramic period sites in the Rosemont area. Irregularly shaped manos are found in small numbers throughout the occupation of the Rosemont area. The second specimen is a vesicular basalt end fragment from a rectangular mano, a common form for the Colonial period and later. Both manos exhibit unifacial use-wear.

Usually handstones are naturally round or oval river cobbles with little or no intentional shaping, which fit comfortably in one hand and are sometimes considered one-handed manos. Handstones were the common grinding implement used by preceramic groups in the Rosemont area (Huckell 1984) but are also present throughout the Hohokam occupation as well (Tagg 1984). Six handstones were recovered, including the one ground stone artifact from AZ EE:2:101. Four are whole specimens and two are fragments. The whole handstones fall well within the size range of handstones from the Rosemont area, with length ranging from 9.8 cm to 11.1 cm, width from 7.9 cm to 9.9 cm, and thickness from 3.9 cm to 4.9 cm. They vary in shape, with two being oval, one round, and one irregular in shape. Only one oval handstone has evidence of intentional shaping, exhibiting a smoothed edge. Two have bifacial use-wear. Material types include unknown igneous (3), quartzite (2), and rhyolitic porphyry (1).

The remaining 15 manos were too fragmentary to place in either category and were categorized only as handstone-mano fragments. The majority of these fragments are probably from handstones rather than manos since they tend to be unshaped river cobble fragments.

Metates

Ten metates were represented in the sample from AZ EE:2:100, including one whole specimen and nine fragments. Metates are the stationary implement in the grinding tool combination and are present in both ceramic and preceramic sites in the Rosemont area. Three types were recognized from Sycamore Canyon depending upon the form of the grinding surface.

Basin metates are those which have had an oval basin worn into one side of a boulder, created by the circular grinding motion of a handstone. Shallow basin metates were used by preagricultural, preceramic groups for grinding seeds, and were used in small numbers in the early phases of the ceramic period (Tagg 1984). Three basin metate fragments were found at AZ EE:2:100, all on relatively flat boulders of vesicular basalt, gabbro, or rhyolitic porphyry. Two of the metates had intentionally flattened bases and the third had a naturally flat base. All three have only incipient to light use wear.

Trough metates are characterized by a rectangular use area and straight walls created by the back-and-forth grinding motion of a two-handed mano. The trough metate with both ends open is the form typical of the Hohokam, and is found from the beginning to the end of the Hohokam record (Haury 1976: 281). One igneous trough metate fragment was found in Feature 1 at AZ EE:2:100. The only remaining end is open, and the metate has light wear, but due to its small size, little else can be said about it.

Flat metates are large, thick boulders with a flat use area covering one entire surface of the boulder. This total coverage would suggest use of a mano whose length matched the width of the metate, although it is also possible that these specimens represent basin or trough metates in their initial stage of use. Three were recovered from AZ EE:2:100, including one complete specimen. Quartzite, an unknown igneous material, and vesicular basalt boulders were used. Wear is incipient on all of the metates, and one fragment has an intentionally flattened base. The whole metate, an igneous boulder measuring 45 cm by 28 cm by 21 cm in size, is interesting because it naturally sits at an angle and has been used bifacially. Metates used at an angle were seen on the Rosemont Hohokam sites, and probably were used at this angle to facilitate the grinding motion (Di Peso 1956: 465). The flat grinding surface of the metate seems to represent the main use area, but the opposite side has seen minimal use in a naturally concave area.

Three additional fragments, all from the grinding surfaces of metates, were too small to place in any of the metate categories.

Pitted Stone

This is a broad category of artifacts that have had a small concavity pecked into one or both surfaces. The exact use of these artifacts is unknown, but they resemble stones used for nutting purposes in the eastern United States, and have also been considered spindle bases and paint grinders (Di Peso 1951: 179, 1956: 402-403). One pecked stone on an igneous cobble fragment was recovered from AZ EE:2:100. It has had the edges ground to produce a round shape, and has a very small, shallow concavity pecked in the center of one side and another possible concavity pecked into the opposing side. No use-wear is apparent in these concavities. Similar artifacts were found on both preceramic and ceramic sites in the Rosemont area (Huckell 1984: 128; Tagg 1984), but the Sycamore Canyon artifact most resembles the more crudely made pitted stones from the Archaic Period sites.

Miscellaneous Ground Stone
_____

One piece of ground stone, a spall from a grinding surface, was too small to determine from what type of tool it came.

Discussion
_____

Although it is very difficult to determine cultural or temporal affiliation of a given site from the ground stone assemblage since many forms of ground stone span long time periods and are present in more than one cultural group or period, some inferences can still be made. A mix of both preceramic and ceramic period ground stone is suggested by the Sycamore Canyon assemblage. Although little can be said about AZ EE:2:101 since only one handstone was recovered, AZ EE:2:100 provided a more substantial collection. The occurrence of a number of unshaped handstones and basin metates suggests an Archaic component, while the recovery of two-handed manos and a trough metate fragment definitely indicates the Hohokam use of the site. However, the handstones and basin metate could also have been used by the Hohokam, but the unshaped nature of the handstones and the higher percentage of basin metates and handstones recovered would indicate predominently Archaic use. The small number of ground stone artifacts indicates that, while plant food processing was occurring in Sycamore Canyon, it was not the sole focus of subsistence activity.

Bone

A total of 85 bone fragments was recovered from AZ EE:2:100, but no bone was found at AZ EE:2:101. Most of the bone recovered was too small to identify more specifically than the size of animal from which it came. That bone which could be identified with some accuracy revealed evidence of deer (Odocoileus sp.), rabbit (Sylvilagus sp.), jack rabbit (Lepus sp.), and squirrel (Sciuridae); six fragments of human bone were also identified. With the exception of the human bone, all these identified fragments are from common animals in the area. The human bone fragments were all burned and calcined (indicating direct contact with flames or hot coals) suggesting evidence of buried cremations that had been disturbed by rodents, roots, or later occupations. All the fragments came from the east half of the site and were associated with sherds in the excavation units, suggesting a Hohokam origin.

Bone fragments which could not be identified more specifically were placed in size classes. A large number (54, or 63.5 percent) of these bone fragments were found to represent medium or large mammals (dog or deer-sized). Of these, only 14 were burned to suggest definite cultural utilization, while the remainder were unburned. Six bone fragments could not be identified even to this broad level.

All the identified bone was from genera common in the area today, and provides no evidence for long range food acquisition. No evidence of butchering marks or bone artifact manufacturing was found. It is interesting to note that, like the ceramics, most of the bone came from the eastern half of the site, suggesting either more cooking and butchering activities occurred on this portion of the site, or that the bone is better preserved with the Hohokam assemblage.

Interpretations

The analysis of the artifacts and features revealed long term, intermittent use of both sites, probably for the seasonal utilization of locally available flora and fauna. Because of this continued periodic use of the sites through time, the artifacts from different occupational episodes are mixed to an unknown degree. In the analysis, an attempt was made to differentiate the various episodes using both the common "diagnostic" artifacts, as well as the less temporally and culturally diagnostic artifacts that are often overlooked.

The artifact assemblages of the two sites were at once different but similar in many ways. Flaked stone dominated the samples, and so formed the major basis for comparison. The assemblages from both sites are alike in the material types used (suggesting locally available material), percentage of debitage types, amount of flake cortex, and flake platform types. They differ, however, in debitage flake size and percentages and types of retouched pieces present. Because the material used for knapping was the same at both sites, this difference in flake size and retouched piece typology and quantity may indicate that different activities occurred at the two sites, or that the intensity of occupation varied. It is obvious that AZ EE:2:100 saw more extensive use than AZ EE:2:101, as indicated by almost seven times more artifacts and at least 60 cm of cultural depth compared to less than 10 cm at AZ EE:2:101. The analysis of the flaked stone assemblages from the Rosemont Hohokam sites indicated that sites which saw heavier use tended to have smaller debitage because material was reduced more intensively than on a site that saw limited use (Rozen 1984). This too, correlates with the results from AZ EE:2:100 and EE:2:101, for the former has more abundant small debitage. However, it would not account for the differences in the numbers and types of retouched pieces. With this in mind, it seems possible that different activities involving different implements and types of reduction were occurring at the two sites. With a high percentage of finely flaked tools such as bifaces and points, and smaller debitage, it is possible that more specialized tool manufacture was done at AZ EE:2:100, which would result in smaller flakes from the soft hammer percussion and pressure retouching. This would also explain why the assemblage was so similar to the Archaic assemblage. Of course, the differences may also be the result of heavier Archaic use of AZ EE:2:100 as opposed to more Hohokam or historic use of AZ EE:2:101, given these same factors. There is no way to determine which of these possibilities produced the differences in the site assemblages due to the degree of admixture of the various cultural and temporal components.

AZ EE:2:100

The analysis of the artifacts from AZ EE:2:100 has indicated preceramic, ceramic, and historic use of the site.

Archaic Period

As mentioned above, the flaked stone assemblage from this site is comparable to the Archaic assemblages in the Rosemont area with its large number of bifaces, projectile points, and small average debitage size. The best indicator of preceramic use of the sites is the large number of clearly Archaic projectile points recovered. Three tapering-stemmed points, though poorly dated, may represent an Early Archaic component suggesting that AZ EE:2:100 may have been occupied as early as 10,500-6800 B.P. Such a date is based on stylistic grounds, principally the formal similarity of this style to Lake Mohave, Jay, and other tapering-stemmed points found in the western United States (Huckell 1984). The Middle Archaic period, roughly dated from 6800 to 3500 B.P., is certainly represented at the site by the recovery of four Pinto style points. These are similar in both formal and material attributes to Pinto points recovered from Rosemont area Archaic sites. Finally, the Late Archaic period (3500 to 1650 B.P.) is thought to be represented by two point styles: the poorly dated large, triangular, concave base style, the most abundant style in the collection with 13 examples, and the more securely dated corner-notched style of dart point. As noted previously, the triangular concave base points have yet to be well dated, but are provisionally included in the Late Archaic period. The occurrence of several handstones and basin metates is also supportive of Archaic use of the site, but these are not entirely dependable temporal indicators.

Ceramic Period

The Hohokam presence at AZ EE:2:100 is indicated by the presence of ceramics, as well as diagnostic projectile points and ground stone tools. A trough metate and two two-handed manos are both Hohokam in origin, occurring throughout the ceramic period but not present in Archaic contexts. The ceramics are the best temporal indicators, and their occurrence mainly on the eastern half of the site suggests that the Hohokam occupied that portion of the ridge remnant most intensively. Of the 257 sherds recovered from this site, 229 were plain ware and 28 were decorated. The plain ware can only be broadly placed in time: Type 1 and Type 2 occur throughout the ceramic period occupation of the Tucson Basin, and Type 3 and Type 4 were dominant during the Rillito phase (A.D. 700-900), but occurred both earlier and later in reduced quantities. The decorated sherds and projectile points are better time indicators, and document Hohokam use of AZ EE:2:100 at least as early as the Rillito phase. The recovery of three small, short, contracting stem arrow points typical of this phase, as well as four Rillito Red-on-brown and two Santa Cruz Red-on-buff sherds are the principal evidence for this occupation. Continued use of the site throughout the Rincon phase (A.D. 900-1200) is indicated by seven Rincon Red-on-brown sherds, but there is no evidence of a Classic period (A.D. 1200-1450) occupation of the site.

All three features on the site are thought to be associated with the Hohokam since they are all located on the east side of the site, and all have sherds associated with them. Feature 1, the large fire-cracked rock scatter which appears to be cleanout from multiple roasting pits or long-term use of a single roasting pit, had 86 sherds in the portion that was excavated. This included one Santa Cruz Red-on-buff and one Rincon Red-on-brown sherd. Feature 2, a small rock-filled pit, had two Type 2 and three Type 3 plain ware sherds in it, and Feature 3, a large roasting pit contained two Type 2 plain sherds and one worked sherd.

Protohistoric-Historic Period

The only evidence of a protohistoric or historic use of the site is a very small, triangular, concave-based, side-notched arrow point typical of the Sobaipuri or Upper Pima Indians. The date of Pima entry into Arizona is a matter of some disagreement, but is presumed to be after A.D. 1450 and before A.D. 1600. Sobaipuri sites in the Rosemont area attest to their use of the Santa Ritas (see Chapter 3). Feature 1 and Feature 3 may also represent historic "mescal" pits since the intrusion of prehistoric artifacts in the fill of a later pit is not unusual, and they are similar to the roasting pit at AZ EE:2:101 which was dated to the historic period.

AZ EE:2:101

Very few diagnostic artifacts came from this site, making the cultural and temporal aspects of its use rather sketchy. The first evidence of use is in the Archaic period, probably the Late Archaic, suggested by the three identifiable points, all the triangular, concave base style so abundant at AZ EE:2:100. The three sherds recovered indicate Hohokam use of the site, with two temporally inspecific Type 2 plain ware sherds and the single Rincon Red sherd that represents the Rincon phase (A.D. 900-1200). The debitage assemblage was also comparable to the ceramic sites debitage assemblages from Rosemont, with large average flake size and typologically similar retouched pieces. However, as with the assemblage from AZ EE:2:100, it must be cautioned that functional rather than temporal factors may have determined these characteristics.

The best temporal evidence from this site came from two radiocarbon dates obtained from Feature 3, the large rock-filled roasting pit. The samples were taken from two separate carbonized branches in the bottom of the pit, and gave very similar results of 140 ± 90 B.P. (A-2933) and 150 ± 90 B.P. (A-2932). These dates would place the feature between A.D. 1700-1900, suggesting use by an historic Indian group. This pit is similar to the ones used historically to roast agave hearts, which were about three feet deep and six feet in diameter. The Apache, Yavapai, and Pima Indians were all known to have used large mescal roasting pits such as this, with Apache features often occurring with definitely non-Apache, prehistoric sites (Gregory 1981: 261; Gifford 1932: 206-7; Russell 1908: 70). Windmiller (1972: 6-20) excavated two "mescal" pits at Ta-e-wun (AZ V:9:13) near Miami, Arizona, which were similar in size and content to the AZ EE:2:101 feature, and thought of protohistoric age. Further, two similar pits were located in the Tonto-Roosevelt area on a Salado site (Gregory 1979: 238-9). The morphology of the AZ EE:2:101 "mescal" pit would suggest a single roasting episode, since multiple roasting episodes tended to leave small mounds of fire-cracked rock (Gregory 1981: 261, Figs. 1a and 1b.

The location of the "mescal" pit on a prehistoric site is not unusual. The Western Apache were known to scavenge and collect artifacts from prehistoric sites in their territory, and the sites were considered sources of desired resources. The fill of the sites would also have been easier to dig in than in nonsite areas, and rocks from features on the sites were readily available for further use (Gregory 1981: 264). The dating of the Apache in the Southwest is problematic, and they are only known to postdate the prehistoric cultures (post-A.D. 1450). While Feature 3 at AZ EE:2:101 is dated, the lack of culturally or temporally diagnostic artifacts associated with it makes it impossible to place the use of the pit with a specific cultural group; however, it is almost certainly attributable to either the Apache or the Papago, given that both groups used the Santa Rita Mountains.

Features 1 and 2, both possible house circles, could not be placed in time due to the total lack of associated diagnostic artifacts. They could represent the remains of temporary bush structures similar to Apache wickiups, or those built by the Papago.

Finally, the recovery of a brown glass vaccine bottle with an aluminum and rubber cap, two Remington-UMC shotshell bases, and a piece of clear glass at AZ EE:2:101 indicate minor Euro-American use of the site within the last 50 years.

Conclusions

The results of the excavations at the Sycamore Canyon sites suggest a long-term, intermittent use of the area, perhaps from the Early through the Late Archaic period, the late Colonial through the Sedentary periods of Hohokam prehistory, and light use in Protohistoric or Historic times. The tops of these lower ridges represent the only areas sufficiently flat and fine grained for habitation in Sycamore Canyon, and the location near a spring makes AZ EE:2:100 and AZ EE:2:101 attractive camping areas. There is no evidence of permanent habitation at either site, although two amorphous rock circle features at AZ EE:2:101 could represent nonpermanent brush shelters on the sites.

All the other features at the sites, including roasting pits and possible hearth areas, as well as the large number of projectile points, ground stone, and bone all point to the exploitation of native flora and fauna in Sycamore Canyon. The occurrence of oak near the sites along the drainages, and agave on the slopes of the canyons present resources which, along with local animals, could have been utilized by the prehistoric and historic inhabitants.

The value of sites such as AZ EE:2:100 and AZ EE:2:101 and other sites like them which have thousands of years of occupation mixed together lies more in the sites themselves. These at least document the specialized exploitation of areas such as Sycamore Canyon by people of a variety of different cultures and temporal periods, and will ultimately aid in describing regional subsistence and settlement patterns.

Chapter 3

SOBAIPURI SITES IN THE ROSEMONT AREA

Bruce B. Huckell

During the survey of the ANAMAX-Rosemont land exchange area in
late 1975, archaeologists encountered two sites that displayed
distinctive oval rock alignments on their surfaces. It was quickly
recognized that these alignments were identical in size and shape to
those reported from protohistoric or early historic Sobaipuri or Upper
Pima sites in the San Pedro (Di Peso 1953; Hammack 1971) and Santa Cruz
(Doyel 1977) river valleys. Both of the newly discovered sites lay
along Barrel Canyon in the northeastern quarter of the proposed exchange
area (Fig. 3.1). At one of these sites, AZ EE:2:80, the Sobaipuri house
rings clearly overlay the remains of a prehistoric Hohokam settlement,
but at the other site, AZ EE:2:83, the Sobaipuri occupation appeared to
be the only component. The presence of Sobaipuri settlements in the
mountainous portion of the northern Santa Rita Mountains was surprising,
for previously known sites occupied by these people were all along the
major river valleys. That they must have used the resources offered by
the mountains was not unexpected, but that actual settlements were
present had not been considered. Both sites, despite relatively
impoverished surface artifact assemblages, were thus deemed to be
potentially significant sources of information about Sobaipuri
subsistence and settlement activities in upland environments.

Plans were made to test these two sites and three others that
lacked house rings but were thought to have Piman brown ware ceramics.
Prior to the 1979 testing phase all these sites were revisited, and it
was found that the three sites without house rings were not of Sobaipuri
or Upper Pima affiliation, but were instead very minor prehistoric
artifact scatters. However, immediately north of AZ EE:2:80 a third
separate locus with a few house rings was discovered; it was designated
AZ EE:2:95 (Fig. 3.1). While its surface artifact assemblage was as
poor as those of its previously discovered counterparts, a large purple
glass bead was located just outside one of the house rings. This was
the first indication that the Sobaipuri had occupied the Rosemont area
after Spanish contact, and so AZ EE:2:95 was added to the list of sites
to be tested.

Accordingly, all three sites were investigated in August of
1979. Each site was mapped, some surface collections were made, and a

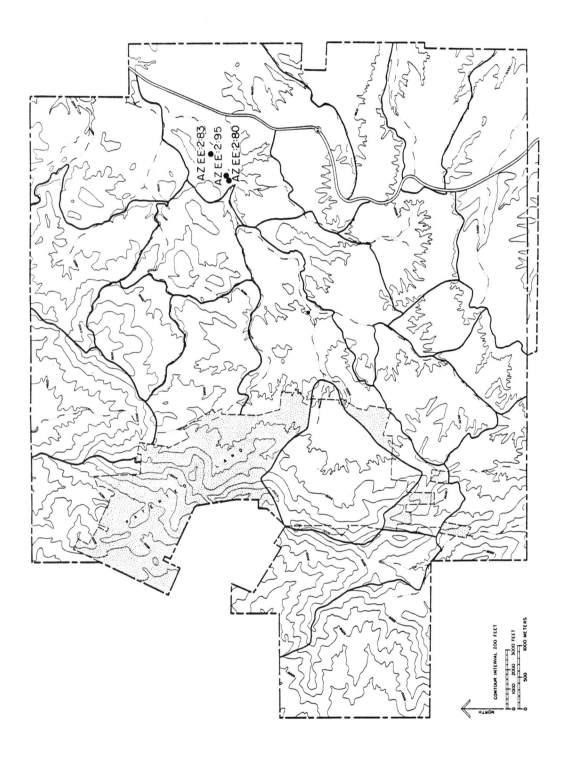

Figure 3.1 Locations of Sobaipuri (Upper Pima) sites in the Rosemont area.

few features and test squares were excavated. The results of this work
were reported in the unpublished testing phase volume (Huckell 1980).
However, in December of 1980, a return visit to AZ EE:2:83 revealed a
cluster of sherds being exposed by erosion outside of one of the tested
features, and two additional artifacts of Spanish origin on the surface.
These latter specimens were mapped in and collected, and the sherd
cluster was excavated. As late as mid-1981 the opportunity to do
intensive excavations at all three sites was eagerly awaited, but in
November of that year word was received that the eastern boundary of the
proposed land exchange area had been redrawn. All three Sobaipuri sites
fell just outside the new boundary, and thus would remain under Coronado
National Forest control.

Although no further work has been done at any of them, it is
believed to be of value to add the testing phase report originally
prepared in 1980 to this volume, so that a published record of these
interesting sites is available. With the addition of the small quantity
of material recovered in 1980 from AZ EE:2:83 and a new introduction and
some editorial changes, this chapter is presented in the same form it
took in the testing phase report (Huckell 1980: 137-160).

AZ EE:2:80

As noted above, AZ EE:2:80 is a dual-component site that lies on
a hill in the middle of Barrel Canyon. The early component is a Rillito
and Rincon phase (A.D. 700-1200) Tucson Basin Hohokam occupation; the
later component is Upper Pima. The hill upon which the site rests could
be aptly described as a 20 m high island in the center of Barrel Canyon.
This hill is basically an erosional remnant of unconsolidated sands and
boulder-sized gravel capped by finer sediments. It has caused the
channel of Barrel Canyon wash to split; the main channel passes to the
east of the hill, although, during periods of heavy discharge, water
will also run down a series of smaller rills to the west of the hill.
Upon the hill itself, a rather disturbed Lower Sonoran plant community
is found, including mesquite trees, white-thorn, prickly pear, ocotillo,
Condalia, and grasses. Scattered juniper trees, normally an Upper
Sonoran element, are also present. Barrel Canyon itself supports a
riparian community dominated in this area by mesquite; occasional oak,
walnut, hackberry, and desert-willow trees are present to the southwest,
further up the canyon.

The Upper Pima component consists of four ovoid structures
outlined by rocks; all were located in the northern two-thirds of the
general site area (Fig. 3.2). These were assigned feature numbers 2
through 5, and one was excavated. No other features were encountered
during the testing phase that could be attributed to the Upper Pima
occupation, nor were any artifacts identified that were of certain Upper
Pima origin. Testing of this component was done in conjunction with,
and as part of, the testing of the site in general. Despite care taken
in both the field and laboratory, it was found that the Upper Pima

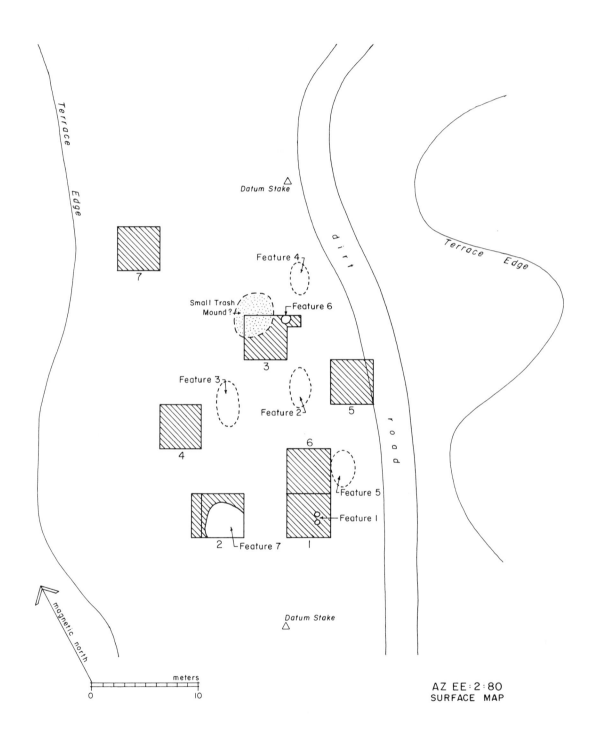

Figure 3.2   Map of AZ EE:2:80.

material culture was simply unrecognizable, if it was indeed present in
the sample. On the basis of observations at the other two sites, it
would appear that artifacts relating to this occupation are, in fact,
quite rare, even at a single-component site. If all of the artifacts
from all of the Upper Pima sites were gathered together, they would
scarcely overflow an 8-pound bag.

Features

Feature 4, the northeasternmost of the four identifiable
structures at AZ EE:2:80, was excavated in an attempt to better define
its original appearance, to locate a floor level, and to enable
comparisons of it with other known Upper Pima structures. Twenty rocks
set vertically into the ground formed the visible outline of the
structure prior to excavation. The feature was excavated entirely by
trowel, and all artifactual material was saved. Table 3.1 and Figure
3.3 present the major attributes of this structure.

Table 3.1.

ATTRIBUTES OF FEATURE 4 AT AZ EE:2:80

Attribute	Description
Type	surface structure
Shape	oval
Length	3.10 m
Width	2.00 m
Depth	surface+
Floor	not found
Wall postholes	not found
Roof-support postholes	not found
Floor pits	none
Hearth	none
Entry way	east wall
Disturbance	cattle?
Age	Protohistoric period

Fill was removed to a depth of 5 cm below modern ground surface.
Generally, this fill was a light grayish brown, gravelly, silty sand
with dispersed larger rock fragments and prehistoric artifacts. No
floor could be defined, nor were any floor features noted. This
dwelling was probably constructed on the ground surface as it existed

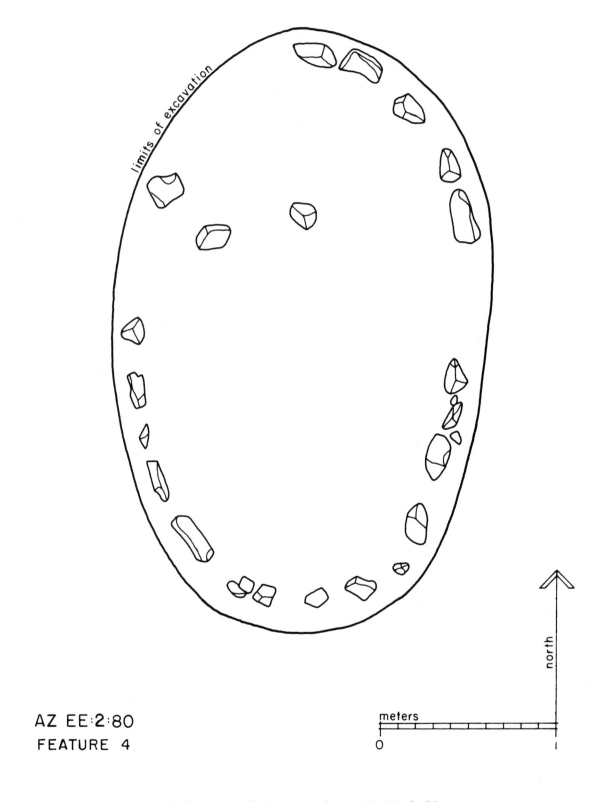

AZ EE:2:80
FEATURE 4

Figure 3.3 Map of Feature 4 at AZ EE:2:80.

when the Upper Pima arrived at the site, at which time this surface and
the underlying 10 cm would have already contained cultural debris from
the earlier Hohokam occupation.

While little can be ascertained of the nature and original
appearance of Feature 4 from the archaeological record, eyewitness
descriptions of such structures were set down by eighteenth-century
Jesuit priests. According to one priest, Ignaz Pfefferkor:,

> The dwellings of the Sonorans are all constructed alike.
> They are approximately the same in size, height, width and
> arrangement, and they are suited in every respect to a people
> whose condition is one of direst poverty. The materials used in
> their construction are tree branches, twigs, and zacaton (a
> plant similar to straw). The branches are cut to a point, and
> this point is driven firmly into the ground. In the middle of
> the house three or four of the branches are made into arches
> equal in height and width. The arches are made lower and
> narrower toward each end until the finished structure assumes
> the shape of a bake oven. Twigs are laid crosswise on the floor
> and are bound to the branches which stand on both sides to make
> the structure durable and firm. Then the entire hut is thatched
> with the aforementioned zacaton in the same way that the houses
> of German peasants are covered with straw. That it may better
> shed rain, the thatch is sprinkled with earth. The diameter of
> the huts is generally not more than four ells, and they are
> hardly three ells high, so that a large man cannot stand inside
> without bowing his head. Some Indians build long huts, one or
> two ells longer than they are wide.

> The door, or round hole, which is the entrance to the
> house is not much larger than the opening to a bake oven, and is
> so low that one must creep through it on hands and knees. The
> Sonoran never thinks of building a window in his house. He can
> well do without this since his most important business is
> slothfulness, which he can carry on without light. The little
> he has to do, he does either outside of the hut or by the meager
> light which enters through the opening (Pfefferkorn 1949: 192).

It is interesting to note that each of the four Upper Pima
structures at AZ EE:2:80 exhibits a long axis oriented generally north-
south. Maps of other Upper Pima sites indicated that such an
orientation is the norm, although many structures will deviate from a
precise north-south alignment by 5 to 30 degrees to either the west or
the east (Di Peso 1953: 62; Hammack 1971: 8; Doyel 1977: 90, 114).
Sizes tend to be consistent as well, as noted by Pfefferkorn. Entries,
where they can be identified, are typically in the east wall.

Artifact Assemblage

As noted above, no artifacts associated with the Upper Pima
occupation were identified during the testing in either grid squares or

features. Feature 4 yielded a total of 16 sherds and 40 flaked stone
artifacts. Fourteen of these sherds were plain ware, but none fitted
the attributes of Whetstone Plain; the remaining two sherds included one
Rincon Red-on-brown sherd and an untypable Tucson Basin red-on-brown
sherd. The flaked stone artifacts consisted of four retouched tools, 13
utilized flakes, and 23 pieces of debitage. At this time it is not
possible to separate Upper Pima flaked stone implements from Hohokam
ones, with the exception of projectile points. Again, the relationship
of these specimens to the structure is dubious. In short, the presence
of the Upper Pima at the site of an earlier Hohokam settlement has
served to obscure the presence of artifacts that might be of Upper Pima
origin.

Summary

The only clear evidence of the late component at AZ EE:2:80
consists of the four oval rock rings that represent the locations of
former Upper Pima houses. Test excavations in one of these and
intensive surface examination of the other three failed to produce any
artifacts of certain Protohistoric period age. Upper Pima reoccupation
of prehistoric sites has been noted elsewhere in the Santa Cruz (Doyel
1977) and the San Pedro valleys (Hammack 1971). It is not surprising to
encounter such a situation here in the Rosemont region, and a second
Upper Pima site, AZ EE:2:83, appears to be a reoccupied Archaic period
locus.

AZ EE:2:95

Approximately 60 m to 70 m north of AZ EE:2:80 and on the
extreme northern end of the same isolated hill lies a cluster of three
oval, rock-ring structure foundations and an exceedingly sparse artifact
scatter (Fig. 3.1). This locus was discovered during the initial visit
to AZ EE:2:80; surface reconnaissance produced a single faceted, purple-
glass bead just outside one of the structures, as well as some flaked
stone debitage and sherds. A decision was made to test the site in
conjunction with work at AZ EE:2:80, although it was given its own site
number (AZ EE:2:95).

As noted, the site lies at the extreme northern end of the flat-
topped, isolated hill. Bounded on the east by a short, headward-cutting
arroyo, it overlooks the floodplain of Barrel Canyon, dominated in this
area by a mesquite bosque. Vegetation on the site is as described for
AZ EE:2:80. Evidence of modern disturbance was limited to a large, 1-m-
deep excavation west of one of the houses and the ubiquitous evidence of
grazing cattle. Figure 3.4 presents a map of the site and its features.
The site was investigated by intensive surface collection, mapping, and
the excavation of one structure. Summer rains prevented more extensive
testing.

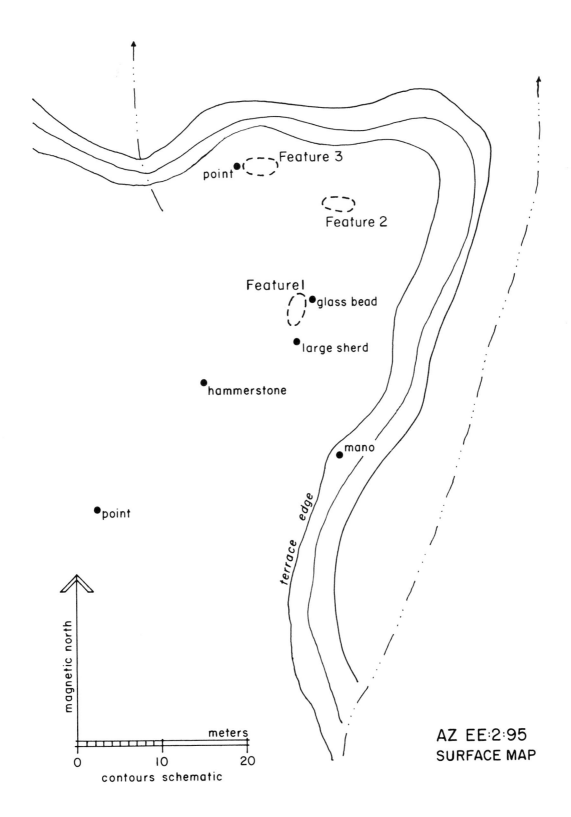

Feature 3

point

Feature 2

Feature1

glass bead

large sherd

hammerstone

mano

point

terrace edge

magnetic north

meters

0   10   20

contours schematic

AZ EE:2:95
SURFACE MAP

Figure 3.4 Map of AZ EE:2:95.

Features

Feature numbers were assigned to the three oval rock rings marking the locations of structures (Fig. 3.4). One of these, Feature 1, was excavated to a depth of 5 cm; its attributes are presented in Table 3.2. The wall foundation stones were set vertically into the ground to form a narrow, ovoid outline whose long axis was aligned northeast to southwest. As was the case for the structure excavated at AZ EE:2:80, no floor could be defined. The fill removed from the interior of the structure was an extremely rocky, gravelly sand that contained two flakes. No hearth, entry, or postholes were located. Sherds and the glass trade bead found earlier lay in close proximity (less than 1 m) to the north and east walls.

Table 3.2.

ATTRIBUTES OF FEATURE 1 AT AZ EE:2:95

Attribute	Description
Type	surface structure
Shape	oval
Length	4.25 m
Width	2.25 m
Depth	surface+
Floor	not found
Wall postholes	not found
Roof-support postholes	not found
Floor pits	none
Hearth	none
Entry way	?
Disturbance	cattle
Age	early Historic Period

The two unexcavated structures are slightly smaller than Feature 1 and lie to the north of it. Both exhibit long axes aligned east to west, parallel to the north edge of the hill (Fig. 3.4); as noted in the discussion of the structures at AZ EE:2:80, most known Upper Pima dwellings are aligned along an essentially north-south axis. Few artifacts were noted near these two structures, although a projectile point (Fig. 3.5c) was recovered from just outside the west wall of Feature 3 by former Coronado National Forest Archaeologist

Don Wood after the close of the testing operation. It was turned over to the Arizona State Museum and added to the collection from the site.

Though not assigned a feature number, the deep excavation to the west of Feature 1 is another prominent part of the site. It was not tested, but visual inspection indicated a lack of artifacts of any kind. Although it was assumed at first to be of relatively recent age, the presence of two similar though much smaller features at AZ EE:2:83 might be cited as possible evidence of greater antiquity. It may, therefore, be of Upper Pima origin, although what purpose it may have served is not immediately apparent. For the time being, it must be noted as a feature of unknown age and function.

Artifact Assemblage

Four sherds, four pieces of flaked stone, a mano, a hammerstone, and a glass bead were recovered during the testing of the site. All of these specimens except one of the flakes were found in surface contexts.

Ceramics

Although only one of the four sherds is larger in diameter than a nickel (about 2 cm), all four are clearly Whetstone Plain, a reddish brown to grayish brown plain ware characterized by a coarse, sandy paste with small amounts (less than 10 percent) of mica and a rough to lightly smoothed surface finish. Vessel walls are thin; the sherds from this site average 3 mm to 4 mm in thickness. Di Peso (1953: 154-156) originally identified and named this type from Quiburi and Santa Cruz de Gaybanipitea, both Sobaipuri (Upper Pima) sites in the San Pedro Valley. He noted that Whetstone Plain was one of two plain ware types to be found at Sobaipuri sites; the other type, Sobaipuri Plain, is much thicker, of poorer quality workmanship, and displays a crudely polished surface finish. Excavations conducted at Upper Pima sites such as Alder Wash Ruin (Hammack 1971) and the England Ranch Ruin (Doyel 1977) produced Whetstone Plain in association with oval, rock-ring house foundations, but failed to yield Sobaipuri Plain. Thus, the two types may not always be associated with one another.

Flaked Stone

Two projectile points, a utilized flake, and an unmodified flake fragment make up the assemblage of flaked stone artifacts recovered from AZ EE:2:95. Both projectile points (illustrated in Fig. 3.5b and c) are simple, concave-based, straight-sided, triangular forms without notches or serrations. Both are made of reddish brown jasper and were produced by extensive pressure flaking. One point (Fig. 3.5c) was found just outside Feature 3, while the other came from 25 m southwest of Feature 1 (Fig. 3.5b). Similar if not identical specimens are reported from Quiburi (Di Peso 1953, Plate 62e) and from the England Ranch Ruin (Doyel 1977, Fig. 73). It may be noted that, at other Upper Pima sites, the

a   b   c

Figure 3.5   Artifacts from AZ EE:2:95.   a, faceted glass bead; b-c, projectile points.

projectile points are often serrated and exhibit very deep basal concavities; this is true of specimens recovered from the Sobaipuri component at the Alder Wash Ruin and from a burial west of Tucson (Brew and Huckell n.d.).   Of interest is Pfefferkorn's assertion that these serrated points were used exclusively on war arrows; arrows used for hunting game bore only fire-hardened, wooden points (Pfefferkorn 1949: 202-203).

The remaining two pieces of flaked stone include one utilized flake with edge damage and a flake fragment.   Both are of locally available metasediment.

Ground Stone

One complete mano, found at the southeastern edge of the site under a small mesquite, represents the only piece of grinding equipment from this locus.   Made from an irregularly ovoid cobble of granite, this specimen shows prominent grinding and pecking marks on one surface and incipient wear on the opposite face.   One end has a small facet produced by pecking and grinding.   Also recovered was a quartzite cobble that had been utilized as a hammerstone.   It displays slight evidence of battering, suggesting only minimal use.

European Trade Item

A single large glass bead (Fig. 3.5a) was located on the surface just a few centimeters outside the northeast end of Feature 1. It is crudely faceted into an irregular octagon and is amethyst-colored. Because of surface pitting and striations, it has a frosted, translucent character. This bead measures 11 mm in width by 9 mm in height, and has a hole 3 mm in diameter. Comparable specimens have been recovered from Navajo burials in the Governador district of New Mexico. Carlson (1965: 91, Fig. 151) and Woodward classified them as "large crude faceted beads", and noted an average diameter of 10.5 mm. The type was further divided into four subclasses on the basis of color: a) colorless, b) milky white, c) amber, and d) blue. The specimen from AZ EE:2:95 may have originally been colorless and have developed its amethyst color after prolonged exposure to the sun's rays. One possible specimen of the blue subclass was recovered from Santa Cruz de Gaybanipitea (Di Peso 1953: 231, Plate 90c), although it was termed a "decagonal" bead. In any case, Woodward suggests an A.D. 1650-1690 date for this type of bead (Carlson 1965: 91).

Summary

AZ EE:2:95 is a small locus occupied by the Sobaipuri or Upper Pima Indians during the early Historic period; the presence of a glass trade bead confirms a post-Spanish contact date for the site. Three house foundations and a sparse scatter of artifacts make up the known features of the locus. AZ EE:2:95 may be part of the Upper Pima occupation of AZ EE:2:80, although nothing was found to demonstrate that the two loci were occupied contemporaneously. The third Upper Pima site lies only 150 m north of AZ EE:2:95; thus, it too may be related.

AZ EE:2:83

Approximately 150 m north of the hill upon which AZ EE:2:80 and AZ EE:2:95 are located lies another hill, situated on the west edge of the Barrel Canyon floodplain (Fig. 3.1). It rises to a height of 20 m above the floodplain, and in shape forms an irregular triangle, with its base oriented east-west. Formed of coarse, poorly consolidated boulder gravel and capped with a lag gravel, it presents a fairly rugged appearance. It was upon the east-facing slope of this hill, however, that the Upper Pima settled.

The hill today supports a sparse vegetative community dominated by mesquite trees, white-thorn, and prickly pear as well as Haplopappus. Because of the presence of a feed trough and salt lick below the site on the floodplain, cattle frequent the site area. The abundant mesquites on the floodplain are also used constantly by cattle for shade and bedding grounds. Modern human disturbance is evidenced by a telephone line that crosses the west end of the hill, a historic horseshoe, and possibly two shallow holes similar to the one noted at AZ EE:2:95.

When found, the site displayed three structure outlines, marked by oval rings of upright rocks, and a very sparse artifact scatter. The testing operation involved three steps. First, a thorough surface collection was made, with all artifacts point-provenienced. Following this, selective excavation of two of the structures, a rock alignment, and one of the shallow holes was conducted. Two test squares were then established in areas devoid of features; only one could be excavated, however, due to the demands of scheduling. Figure 3.6 presents a map of the site, its features, and the locations of the units tested.

Features

Eight archaeological constructions, including four apparent structures, two rock alignments, and the two depressions were assigned feature numbers. Four of these features (two structures, a rock alignment, and one of the depressions) were partially or completely exposed by excavation.

The attributes of the two excavated structures, Features 1 and 3, are presented in Table 3.3; Feature 1 is illustrated in Figure 3.7. Both houses exhibit long axes oriented north-south; Feature 1, however, is a much narrower, more elongated dwelling than Feature 3. Feature 1 also yielded identifiable Upper Pima sherds inside its walls, as well as a few flakes and three fragments of a tabular slate knife. An apparent hearth, marked by a concentration of eight rocks, was present just north of the center of Feature 1 (Fig. 3.7). As mentioned previously, such features are occasionally present in Upper Pima houses (Hammack 1971: 8; Doyel 1977: 113-114); Pfefferkorn, in fact, noted that Upper Piman structures had hearths in them (Pfefferkorn 1949: 193). An additional test square excavated east of, but contiguous, to Feature 1 produced a possible trivet of large rocks as well as numerous potsherds and the tip of an iron knife blade.

Results of the excavation of Feature 3 were more consistent with those obtained from tested structures at AZ EE:2:80 and AZ EE:2:95. No hearth or other features were defined, and the entire artifact assemblage from inside the structure consisted of three potsherds. However, outside the northeastern corner of the structure a cluster of badly broken sherds were found in December of 1980. Excavation of this cluster covered a 1-square-meter area, and resulted in the recovery of 98 small sherds, 2 flakes, and 2 tiny fragments of calcined bone.

A rock alignment at the northeastern end of the site was investigated through excavation of a rectangular test pit measuring 3 m by 6 m (Fig. 3.6); this alignment was designated Feature 2. It was almost completely straight, bowing only slightly toward the east, and resembled a structure wall in its construction. A few sherds were found within the excavated area, and a large cluster of over 70 badly crushed sherds occurred on the surface approximately 4 m east of the alignment. No clear indications of the function of this alignment were obtained from testing; it may represent some sort of windbreak to protect a work area, or it may be a wall of an unfinished or demolished structure.

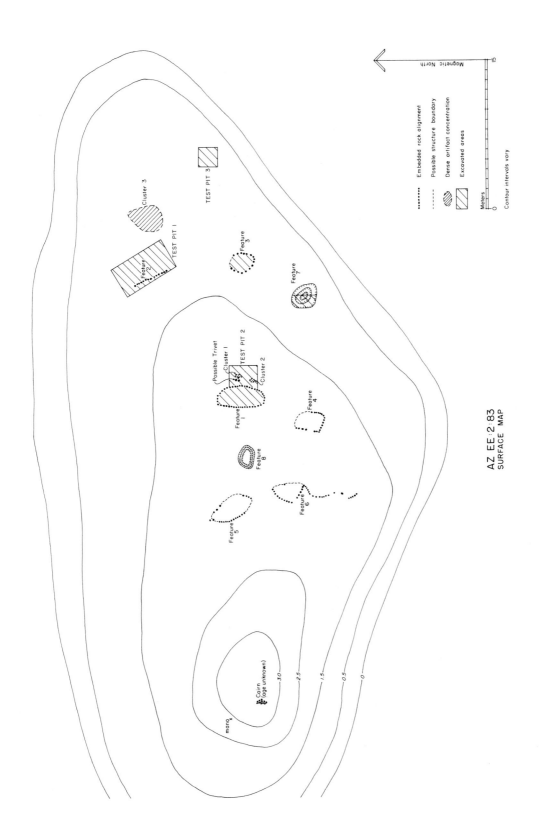

AZ EE:2:83
SURFACE MAP

Figure 3.6 Map of AZ EE:2:83.

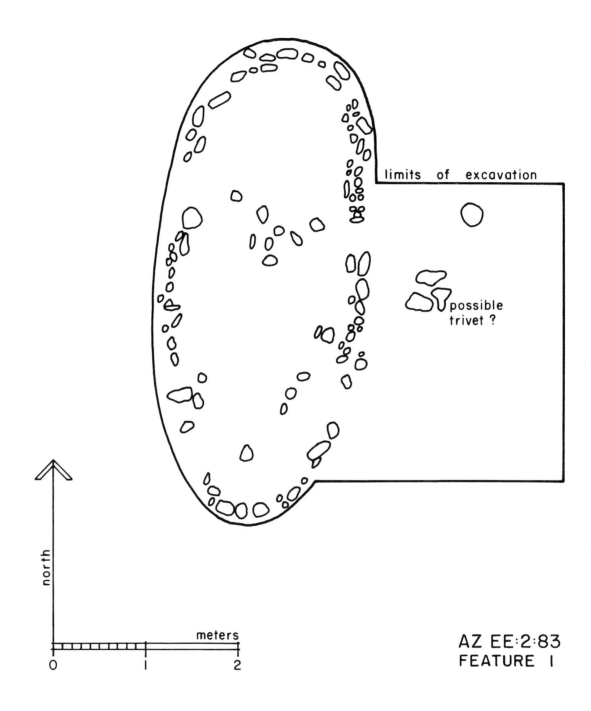

limits of excavation

possible
trivet ?

north

meters

0   1   2

AZ EE:2:83
FEATURE 1

Figure 3.7 Map of Feature 1 at AZ EE:2:83

Table 3.3.

ATTRIBUTES OF STRUCTURES AT AZ EE:2:83

	Feature 1	Feature 3
Type	surface structure	surface structure
Shape	oval	oval
Length	5.00 m	3.70 m
Width	2.25 m	2.50 m
Depth	surface+	surface+
Floor	not found	not found
Wall postholes	not found	not found
Roof support postholes	not found	not found
Floor pits	none	none
Hearth	rock cluster	none
Entry way	?	?
Disturbance	cattle	cattle
Age	early Historic period	early Historic period

Cross sectioning of one of the small depressions (Feature 7; see Fig. 3.6) revealed a pit with initially shallow, sloping sides that dipped sharply to form a steep-sided, hemispherical pit in its lower half or two-thirds (Fig. 3.8). Two separate strata were apparent: an upper unit of light brown, gravelly sand, and a lower unit of dark brown to grayish brown, gravelly sand with numerous rocks ranging from 5 cm to 7 cm in diameter. None of the rocks appeared to be fire-cracked, nor was any ash or charcoal observed in either unit. Three pieces of flaked stone were recovered from the screened fill of the pit. No simple explanation of the function of this pit may be readily offered. If it functioned as a cooking pit, its use was of short duration, and it was cleaned out after its last use. As described by Pfefferkorn (1949: 199-200), agave was utilized as a foodstuff by the Upper Pima, and there is, in fact, a supply of this plant on a high ridge immediately northwest of the site; the lack of evidence of burning, however, renders this explanation of the pit's function questionable. It may be that this pit is not of Upper Piman origin, and that it is some type of more recent test pit, although the nature of the fill and the presence of artifacts in the upper unit might indicate otherwise.

Artifact Assemblage

AZ EE:2:83 yielded a much larger artifact assemblage than either AZ EE:2:80 or AZ EE:2:95, although it still could not be regarded as

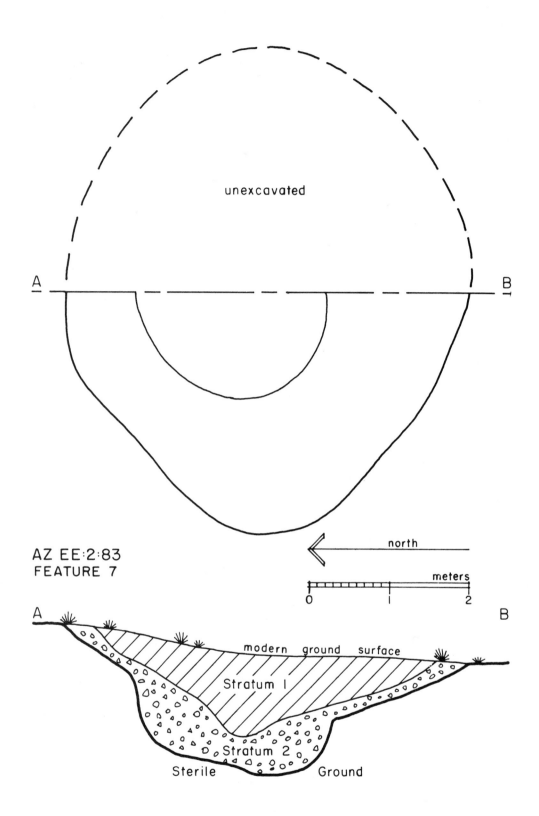

AZ EE:2:83
FEATURE 7

Figure 3.8 Plan and cross section for Feature 7 at AZ EE:2:83.

sizable. Nevertheless, 223 sherds, 47 pieces of flaked stone, 4 ground stone artifacts, an iron knife fragment, a fragmentary glass bead, and a rolled sheet brass tinkler were recovered.

Ceramics

All but two of the 223 sherds from the site appear to be readily assignable to Whetstone Plain. Only 61 sherds (27.6 %) are technically large enough to be termed "classifiable"; the remaining 160 sherds (72.4%) are less than 2 cm in diameter and, for the sake of consistency, have been placed in a "too small" category. In all likelihood, cattle have been a major factor in the extreme degree of breakage at this site. In any event, no differences in paste, temper, color, or surface finish were observed between the sherds assigned to the two categories. Three small rim sherds, all from jars, represent the only firm evidence of vessel forms present at the site.

Two sherds were recovered from the floor of Feature 1 during December of 1980 that appear to be much more like Sobaipuri Plain (Di Peso 1953: 147-151) than any others from the site. They are relatively thick (8 mm), display a dark gray, organic core, and bear a lightly smoothed, irregular exterior surface. The exterior surface color is a dull reddish brown. Both sherds are provisionally assigned to the Sobaipuri Plain type.

Flaked Stone

As Table 3.4 indicates, 27 flaked stone implements were identified, including 12 utilized flakes and 15 retouched tools; these represent 60 percent of the total flaked stone assemblage. Thirteen unmodified waste flakes and five cores round out the assemblage.

The retouched tools include five scrapers, a graver, and nine miscellaneous unifacially and bifacially retouched tools. Analysis casts extreme doubt upon their association with the Upper Pima ceramics and architecture. As Table 3.4 shows, all the scrapers, the graver, and all but two of the miscellaneous unifacially or bifacially retouched tools are of either chert or metasediment; in addition, all display obvious patina on their surfaces. In form, raw material, and surface alteration, these implements closely resemble artifacts recovered from the Archaic period sites. Thus, the Protohistoric occupation apparently overlies a much earlier Archaic component. The absence of projectile points makes it difficult to date this early component, but typological similarities to the Middle Archaic artifacts recovered from AZ EE:2:62 and AZ EE:2:82 may be noted.

The utilized flakes probably include Upper Pima artifacts. Note that all but one of these are either of quartzite or metasediment, in distinct contrast to the retouched tools (Table 3.4). In addition, most of these specimens do not bear the patina found on the retouched implements. If comparative groupings are sought, they may be found in

TABLE 3.4

FLAKED STONE ARTIFACTS
FROM AZ EE:2:83

Material Type

Artifact Type	Quartzite	Chert	Metasediment	Chalcedony	Jasper	Total
Debitage	4(26.7)	2(13.3)	7(46.7)	1(6.7)	1(6.7)	15(100.0)
Primary decortication	2					2(13.3)
Secondary decortication			1			1(6.7)
Tertiary decortication	2	1	2	1	1	7(46.7)
Biface thinning			2			2(13.3)
Tool retouch		1				1(6.7)
Shatter			2			2(13.3)
Utilized flakes	5(41.7)		6(50.0)	1(8.3)		12(100.0)
Decortication, polished	3					3(25.0)
Decortication, damaged	2		6	1		9(75.0)
Retouched flakes	1(6.7)	8(**53.3**)	5(33.3)		1(6.7)	15(100.0)
Unifacially retouched	1	2	1			4(26.7)
Bifacially retouched		2	2		1	5(33.3)
Scrapers		3	2			5(33.3)
Gravers		1				1(6.7)
Cores	1(20.0)		4(80.0)			5(100.0)
Multiplatform	1					1(20.0)
Globular			2			2(40.0)
Fragmentary			2			2(40.0)

( ) = Percent of type

the flaked stone assemblages recovered from the prehistoric Hohokam sites.

Of the five cores, three are sufficiently complete to classify; one is a multiple platform core, and two are globular cores. The globular cores and two core fragments are of metasediment, while the multiple platform specimen is of quartzite.

The unmodified flakes from the site comprise an interesting and varied group (Table 3.4). In terms of raw materials, metasediment and quartzite predominate, as might be expected at a Hohokam site. In terms of flake types, however, the higher percentages of primary and secondary decortication flakes, biface-thinning flakes, and tool-retouch flakes are notable. This amount of variation in flake types within such a small collection is unusual.

Ground Stone

Two manos, a hammerstone, and parts of a tabular knife constitute the ground stone artifacts from the site. Both of the manos are simple quartzite cobbles that show evidence of pecking and grinding on both surfaces. One cobble is an elongated oval in shape and exhibits what appear to be rust stains on one surface. The other is a subrectangular to square cobble. Both are quite heavy and bear evidence of relatively short-term use.

The hammerstone is quite similar to the specimen from AZ EE:2:95. It is a simple quartzite cobble that bears evidence of slight hammering activity in the form of pits on one prominence. It may have functioned as a hammer for flaking rather than for pecking.

Finally, four pieces of a grayish green, tabular slate knife were found in and near Feature 1. Three of these pieces fit together, but the fourth cannot be attached, although it is certainly from the same specimen. Shaped by grinding, this knife bears one thin, denticulated cutting margin. It is identical to tabular knives recovered from prehistoric Hohokam sites in southern Arizona (see Greenleaf 1975: 96). Whether this item is of Upper Pima manufacture or was secured from a prehistoric site is not known; tools of this type are generally not considered to be characteristic of Upper Pima material culture.

European Trade Items

The broken tip of an iron knife blade (Fig. 3.9c) was recovered from subsurface context approximately 1 m east of Feature 1. It was associated with several sherds of Whetstone Plain, and is therefore believed to be related to the Upper Pima occupation of AZ EE:2:83. This tip, part of a very thin-bladed knife, probably broke off when the knife was being used in a prying capacity. Simmons and Turley (1980: 130-132, Plates 22 and 23) discuss and illustrate what is termed a belduque or peasant knife; this knife shows a thin, graceful point very reminiscent of the recovered specimen. Iron knives were in great demand among the

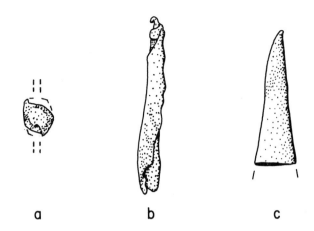

Figure 3.9 Artifacts of European manufacture from AZ EE:2:83.
a, faceted glass bead; b, rolled sheet brass tinkler; c, tip
fragment of an iron knife blade.

Upper Pima, as is evidenced by Pfefferkorn's comments on stealing and
trading (1949: 197, 198). Complete and fragmentary examples of various
forms of knives have been found at Quiburi (Di Peso 1953, Plates 72 and
75), Santa Cruz de Gaybanipitea (Di Peso 1953, Plate 90), and San
Cayetano del Tumacacori (Di Peso 1956, Plate 7a).

Two other artifacts indicative of Spanish contact were found on
the surface of this site in December of 1980. The first of these is a
fragmentary faceted bead of translucent blue glass. In form it appears
to be identical to the "decagonal" bead of amethyst-colored glass
recovered from AZ EE:2:95, and would likely have been of similar size as
well. In its present condition it represents slightly less than half of
the bead, having been split through the center in a plane roughly
parallel to the hole (Fig. 3.9a). Di Peso (1953, 206: Fig. 79i, upper)
reported apparently identical beads from Quiburi.

The second artifact is of Spanish sheet brass, but may be of Upper
Pima manufacture. As shown in Figure 3.9b, it is a piece of sheet brass
that has been rolled to form a cylindrical shape; careful inspection of
the drawing will show that the upper end has been bent to form a crude
eye. Presumably this specimen is designed to be attached to clothing, a
necklace, or perhaps a basket to serve as a tinkler. Once again,
Di Peso (1953, Fig. 24) hasidentified such items from Quiburi.

Summary

AZ EE:2:83 is the largest of the Upper Pima sites in the Rosemont
area, and also contains the largest assemblage of artifacts. Test
excavations reveal that, like AZ EE:2:95, this site may be dated to the

early Historic period, after initial Spanish contact with the native population. In addition, the testing documented traces of an earlier Archaic period occupation at the same locus.

Discussion

The limited testing carried out in 1979 at these three sites has served to demonstrate that the Sobaipuri or Upper Pima called the Rosemont area their home for a short time during the late Protohistoric and early Historic periods. Spanish trade goods recovered from AZ EE:2:95 and AZ EE:2:83 clearly demonstrate that these sites were occupied during the period of early Spanish contact, and it is not inconceivable that the Upper Pima component at AZ EE:2:80 is also of early Historic period age. A rough time estimate of A.D. 1650-1780 may be postulated for this group of sites. The early end of this estimate is based upon the apparently early glass trade beads from AZ EE:2:95 and AZ EE:2:83; the later end is based upon the upsurge of Apache raiding during the 1760s and 1770s. The Apache began to force the Upper Pima known as the Sobaipuri out of the San Pedro River Valley at about A.D. 1700 (Di Peso 1953: 30-32), and by the 1760s and 1770s, Apache raiding pressure on the Santa Cruz River settlements had increased markedly. During this time, the Sobaipuri from the San Pedro Valley were settling with their kinsmen along the Santa Cruz or moving southward into Mexico, and would have been less likely to venture into the Santa Rita Mountains. Evidence from the Rudo Ensayo indicates that the Sobaipuri had left the San Pedro Valley for good by 1764 (Nentvig 1980: 73). By 1780, the presidio at Quiburi had been abandoned for the last time by the Spanish, who withdrew to positions farther west.

It might also be noted that during the Pima Revolt of 1751 certain groups of the Sobaipuri from Santa Maria Soamca in what is now northern Sonora fled to the Santa Rita Mountains (Di Peso 1956: 61). This suggests that they were already familiar with this range and with the resources that it offered. In fact, it is not inconceivable that these three sites were occupied by Pima refugees during all or part of the five month long revolt.

Regardless of its exact date, it seems clear that the Sobaipuri occupation of the Rosemont area was relatively brief, as indicated by the extremely low artifact densities at all three sites. It would certainly not have taken long to construct the houses at each of the sites; assuming access to all of the necessary building materials, a house of the Upper Pima type can be erected in a few hours. The length of the entire occupation at any of these sites is difficult to estimate, but is probably best calculated in weeks rather than in months.

The activities undertaken at the sites and the resources that attracted people to the Rosemont area are difficult to pinpoint at this time. Floodwater farming may have been undertaken along Barrel Canyon, although assuming that the large river valleys were accessible, this may not have been too likely. The availability of mountain resources, including acorns, walnuts, agave, and deer, may be proposed as a more likely attraction. While some of these resources can be found at lower elevations, they are more concentrated in this area. The three sites discussed here, however, are located away from the modern concentrations of oak and walnut trees. This problem clearly requires further research, and these sites may yet be of more help in ascertaining the nature of Upper Pima subsistence activities outside the river valleys.

Chapter 4

RESIDENTIAL TERRACES AT AZ EE:1:91
A LATE RINCON/EARLY TANQUE VERDE SITE IN THE SANTA RITAS

Martyn D. Tagg

In 1980, the ANAMAX Mining Company proposed that two additional parcels of land be included in the ANAMAX-Rosemont land exchange. The two parcels, consisting of approximately 320 acres each, were located on the southwestern and western border of the main project area. Archaeological survey of these parcels by Arizona State Museum archaeologists located one prehistoric and three historic sites (Huckell 1981). The prehistoric site (AZ EE:1:91), located on the western edge of the exchange area, was tested during the excavation of the Hohokam sites in the Rosemont area because it was thought that the site might provide information on the use of specific topographic situations and biotic communities outside the Barrel Canyon area. Because the site was located in an environment quite distinct from the Rosemont area, and contained architectural features unlike any seen on sites there, it was handled as an investigation separate from the main work in the Barrel Canyon area (Ferg and others 1984). This report presents a description of AZ EE:1:91 and its artifact assemblage, as well as a discussion of the temporal and functional aspects of the site.

Environment

The site is located on the western border of the proposed exchange area, separated from the Rosemont area by the ridgeline of the Santa Rita Mountains (Fig. 4.1). It lies approximately 2.2 km east-southeast of the site of Helvetia, a former mining camp of the late nineteenth and early twentieth centuries. The west-facing slopes in this area consist of major northwest-southeast trending ridges incised and drained by deeply cut canyons. The steeper slopes have bedrock exposures of Precambrian granite, Cretaceous sedimentary rocks, and Tertiary-Cretaceous intrusive igneous dikes and sills; below these are slopes of colluvial and alluvial gravel and sand deposits. The bulk of this area contains typical Lower Sonoran life zone vegetation consisting mainly of ocotillo (Fouquieria splendens), mesquite (Prosopis juliflora), mesquitilla and other shrubs, cholla and prickly pear

131

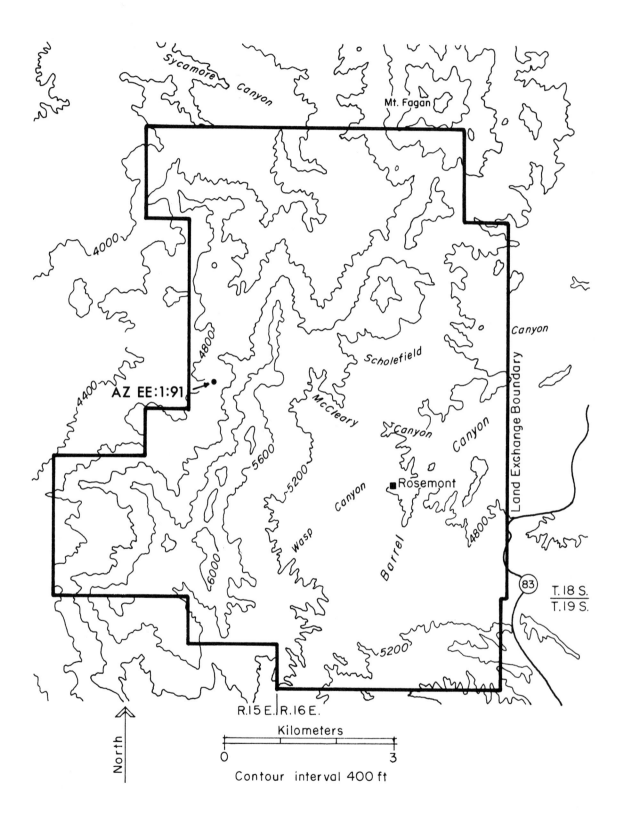

Figure 4.1 Map showing the location of AZ EE:1:91 within the
ANAMAX-Rosemont land exchange area.

(<u>Opuntia</u> sp.), and a ground cover of annual grasses. To the south is an unnamed canyon with vegetation more common in the Upper Sonoran life zone such as oaks (<u>Quercus</u> spp.), one-seed juniper (<u>Juniperus</u> <u>monosperma</u>), beargrass (<u>Nolina</u> <u>microcarpa</u>), yucca, mimosa, and grasses, as well as abundant mesquite and cacti. Oak and hackberry trees line the ephemeral canyon drainages (Huckell 1981: 3).

Site Description

AZ EE:1:91 is located on the relatively steep slope of an east-west trending colluvial fan or ridge, ranging in elevation from 4880 feet to 4920 feet. A large wash runs along the northern border of the site, and on-site vegetation consists of mesquite, Mexican blue oak, mimosa, beargrass, yucca, various cacti, smaller perennial plants, and annual grasses. Recent cultural disturbance associated with mineral exploration includes three primitive roads cut through portions of the site and two large bulldozed areas at the southern edge of the site (Huckell 1981: 3). Natural disturbance consists mainly of heavy sheetwashing caused by the steepness of the slope.

The site consists of eight rock-bordered platforms or terraces and a very sparse scatter of surface artifacts in an area 40 m north-south by 160 m east-west (Fig. 4.2). The platforms exhibit either a semicircular or three sided rectangular border of rocks, open on the upslope side, and creating a level bench on the steep slope of the ridge. The platforms range in size from 4.5 m to 8 m long and from 2.5 m to 6.5 m wide. The borders consist of angular, unmodified, locally available quartzite and granite boulders and cobbles, and range from one to two courses (30 cm to 40 cm) in height.

Because only a small amount of time could be spent at this site, the field strategy was very simple, consisting of mapping the complete site area and investigating two of the platform features. One feature, which had been minimally disturbed by one of the bulldozer cuts, was chosen for complete excavation because the disturbance revealed a dark fill with artifacts. A second platform, chosen because of the good condition and completeness of the rock border, also had a 1 m by 2 m unit placed within it. The earth was removed in a single level using picks, shovels, pickmattocks, and trowels, and all excavated fill was passed through one-quarter inch mesh screens.

Feature 1

Feature 1 is a cleared area with a semicircle of rocks bordering the down slope side of the clearing, measuring approximately 6 m north-south by 8 m east-west (Fig. 4.3). The south edge of the feature had been disturbed by a bulldozer cut and a pile of backdirt was deposited on the southeast corner. The complete excavation of this feature revealed the floor of a structure lying level with the top course of

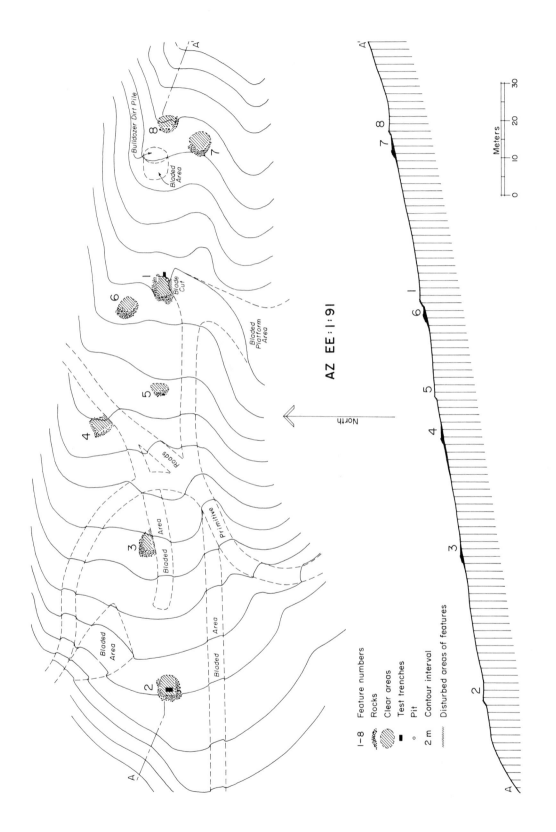

AZ EE:1:91

Figure 4.2 Map of AZ EE:1:91.

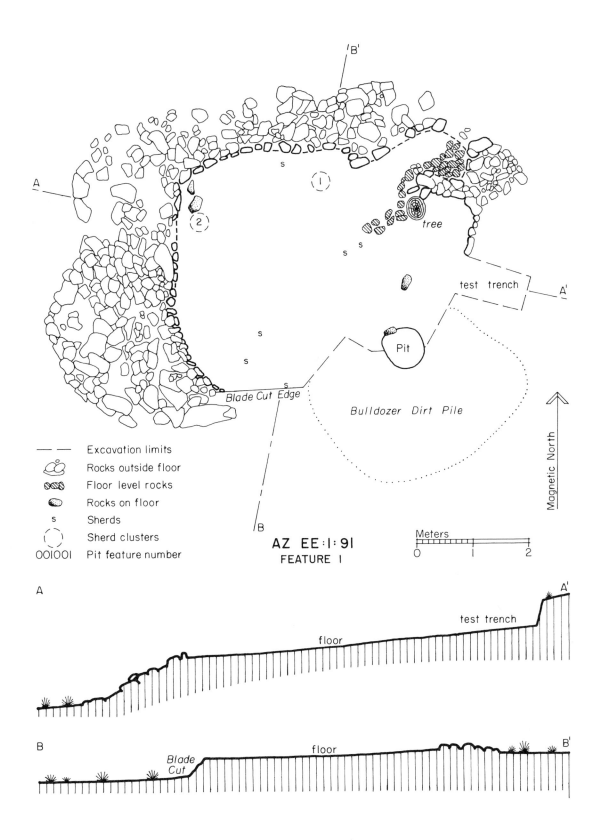

Excavation limits
Rocks outside floor
Floor level rocks
Rocks on floor
s   Sherds
Sherd clusters
OOIOOI   Pit feature number

AZ EE:1:91
FEATURE 1

Meters
0   1   2

Magnetic North

Figure 4.3 Map of Feature 1 at AZ EE:1:91.

border rocks. The floor of the structure is relatively flat, rising slightly towards the uphill side (Fig. 4.3), and consisted of sterile reddish brown sand. Several sherd clusters were found on the floor, including two secondary vessels, and a possible subfloor pit was located and excavated in the southeast corner of the house. The pit was 75 cm in diameter and 16 cm deep, but its exact shape was difficult to determine due to heavy rodent disturbance. No other floor features were found. The exact size, shape, or type of structure could not be determined due to the disturbed nature of the south side of the feature and the indistinct floor on the east edge.

Feature 2

Feature 2 is a relatively square platform of rocks with the uphill side open, and a cleared area in the center measuring 6 m north-south by 7 m east-west. This feature is located 105 m west and downslope of Feature 1. A 1-m-by-2-m test unit was placed in the southwest corner of the feature and excavated to a flat, sterile surface which was interpreted as the house floor. Unlike Feature 1, the floor of this house is 40 cm below the top course of the border rocks and this feature probably represents a pit house.

The six unexcavated features varied in morphology, with one (Feature 4) being very similar to Feature 2, and the remaining five having semicircular terraces more like Feature 1.

Artifact Assemblage

A total of 219 artifacts was recovered from the excavations of the two features at AZ EE:1:91, including 3 partially reconstructed secondary or reworked vessels, 197 sherds, 20 flaked stone specimens, and 1 piece of ground stone (Table 4.1). Because of the small number of artifacts, the analysis was designed only to offer a description of the assemblage in an attempt to place the site temporally, and perhaps determine its function. For the analysis, the artifacts were divided into three categories: ceramics, flaked stone, and ground stone. Two pollen samples and a flotation sample from Feature 1 were also analyzed.

Ceramics

All the ceramics recovered from AZ EE:1:91 were common Tucson Basin types. Table 4.2 illustrates their distribution on the site.

Plain Ware

Undecorated, unslipped plain ware made up the bulk of the ceramic assemblage with 164 sherds (74.9%). Of these, 41 (25% of the

Table 4.1

DISTRIBUTION OF ARTIFACTS FROM AZ EE:1:91

Artifact Class	Feature 1	Feature 2	Total
Ceramics	178[1]	19[2]	197
Flaked Stone	19	1	20
Ground Stone	1		1
Total	198	20	218

[1] Includes 2 secondary vessels
[2] Includes 1 secondary vessel

plain ware) were too badly eroded to be identified as to type. The remaining 122 sherds were all identified as Type 2 plain ware as defined by Deaver (1984) based on the technology and surface finish of the pottery. Type 2 is a paddle and anvil constructed, lightly micaceous brown ware with sand temper and a smoothed surface finish. Surface color ranges from orangish brown to dark brown and gray, and fire clouding of surfaces is common. Type 2 plain ware occurs throughout the Hohokam occupation of the Rosemont area, from the Canada del Oro through the late Rincon phases, and is the dominant plain ware in all phases except the Rillito phase. It is also thought to occur in the Classic period based on comparisons with plain ware from Classic sites in the Tucson Basin.

Type 2 sherds were recovered from both excavated features, and included a sherd collected from the surface of another terrace, Feature 3. Only five rim sherds were present in the collection, four from jars and one from a bowl. The most interesting aspect of the plain ware was the recovery of three partially reconstructable, reworked vessels. Broken portions of larger vessels had been reworked for a secondary purpose by grinding and smoothing the broken edges. Two of the vessels were found together on the floor of Feature 1 (the sherd cluster in Fig. 4.3). One is a little less than half of a medium-sized jar (24.5 cm in diameter and 7.5 cm deep) which has been made into a bowl, with a portion of the rim remaining as a handle (Fig. 4.4a). The second, a 12.8 cm by 9.1 cm piece from the lower portion and base of a jar, has been reworked into what appears to be a small scoop (Fig. 4.4b). A third vessel (Fig. 4.4c), recovered from the fill of

Table 4.2

DISTRIBUTION OF CERAMICS BY FEATURE AT AZ EE:1:91

Pottery Type	Feature Number 1	2	Total	Percent
Rincon Red-on-brown, Style B		1	1	0.5
Rincon Red-on-brown, Style C	1		1	0.5
Rincon Red-on-brown, Style ?		4	4	2.0
Rincon Red-on-brown, smudged	2		2	1.0
Tanque Verde Red-on-brown	2		2	1.0
Unidentified Red-on-brown	31		31	15.7
Plain ware, Type II	103[1]	12[2]	115	58.4
Plain ware, unidentified	39	2	41	20.8
Total	178	19	197	

[1] Includes 1 partial vessel
[2] Includes 2 partial vessels

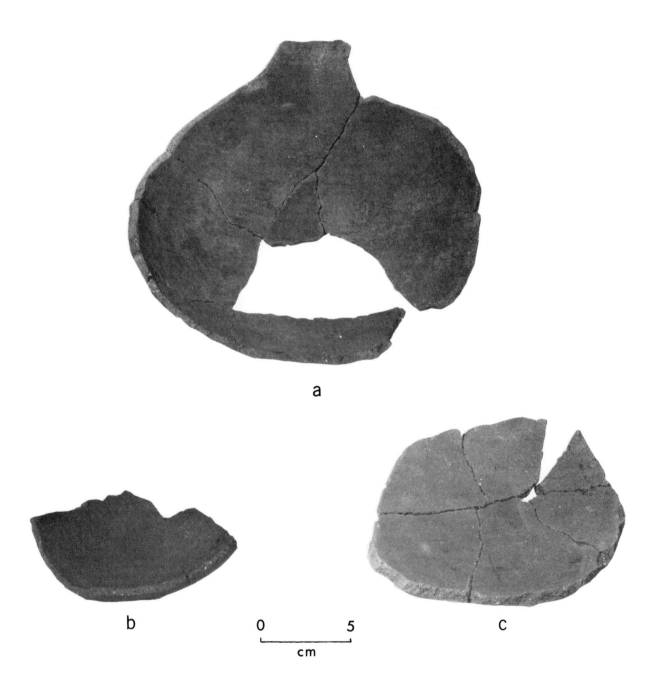

Figure 4.4   Three reworked, secondary vessels from AZ EE:1:91.   <u>a</u>, large
jar sherd reworked into a bowl; <u>b</u>, reworked large sherd, possibly a scoop;
<u>c</u>, large sherd reworked into a discoidal form.

Feature 2, is roughly oval in shape, 16 cm by 14.2 cm in size, and resembles the smaller sherd disks found in the Rosemont area. While smaller disks are thought to be gaming pieces or jar lids, the use of this larger type is probably for some utilitarian purpose such as a small plate or palette. These artifacts fall into the secondary vessel category, defined by Deaver (1984) as partial vessels reworked into a different form. Examples from the Rosemont area included jars made into bowls, bowls made into plates, and small vessel fragments made into scoops, palettes, or disks. Deaver noted that most of the vessels found on house floors in the Rosemont area were these forms, suggesting that the reuse of these fragments and other secondary vessels was common.

Decorated Ceramics

A total of 41 decorated sherds was recovered from AZ EE:1:91, of which only 10 (24.4%) could be identified as to type. The remaining 31 were too eroded to identify beyond the Tucson Basin red-on-brown category.

Eight Rincon Red-on-brown sherds were found, representing the earliest identified pottery type on the site; it spans the Sedentary period of Hohokam prehistory (A.D. 900-1200). Surface color ranges from orangish brown, to brown, to dark gray, and surfaces are usually fire clouded, indicating a lack of control of the firing atmosphere. Sand is the dominant temper type; by the middle Sedentary period, schist is not used at all and Rincon Red-on-brown can be recognized by the lack of mica. Three different varieties of Rincon Red-on-brown were recognized from the Rosemont area (Deaver 1984), only two of which were seen at AZ EE:1:91. Style B emphasizes a gridlike design pattern using small geometric spaces, and either triangles, rectangles, or diamonds to subdivide the decorative field. A large number of design elements are seen, with many decorative units being used in a single design. This type of decorative treatment is the hallmark for the middle Sedentary period (A.D. 1000-1100). Rim lips are always painted, the brushwork is refined, and the draftsmanship is improved from earlier periods (Deaver 1984). One Style B smudged bowl rim was recovered from Feature 2. Smudging of bowl interiors, which sometimes partially or completely obscures the decoration, was common in this period.

Style C is similar to Style B in decorative structure, although the designs are more simple and there is a greater use of open space. It has also been called Cortaro Red-on-brown, and is present in the late Rincon period (A.D. 1100-1200). A Style C jar sherd was found in Feature 1.

The remaining six Rincon sherds could not be identified to a particular style due to their deteriorated state. Four jar sherds from Feature 2 were identified only as Rincon Red-on-brown, and two bowl rims from Feature 1 were called Rincon Red-on-brown, smudged variety.

Tanque Verde Red-on-brown marks the beginning of the Classic period and was manufactured throughout that time period (A.D. 1200-

1450). Surface color of sherds is similar to that of Rincon Red-on-brown with a tendency towards a pronounced orange cast. Fire clouding continues and interior smudging of bowls is prevalant. The main decorative field is almost always on the exterior of bowls and jars, with interior rim designs not uncommon. Design elements are usually in a horizontal band that encircles the exterior of the vessel. Typical design elements are crosshatch-filled elements, interlocking rectangular scrolls, barbed lines, and opposing flagged lines (Kelly 1978: 48-54; Tagg 1983: 17). Two Tanque Verde Red-on-brown jar sherds were recovered from Feature 1, and exhibited the opposing flagged line design. In a recent conversation, Bill Deaver indicated that the sherds appeared to be stylistically, and thus probably temporally, early in the Tanque Verde phase.

Flaked Stone

Only a small quantity of flaked stone was recovered from AZ EE:1:91, including a possible scraper, a hammerstone, two cores, and 16 pieces of debitage (Table 4.3). With the exception of the hammerstone, all this material was from Feature 1. The 16 pieces of debitage consisted of seven complete flakes, four flake fragments with striking platforms, and five fragments without platforms (for definition of terms and analysis techniques, see Chapter 2). Flake size was generally large, with 13 of the 16 pieces larger than 2 cm in maximum dimension. Most flakes had little cortex, with 13 of the 16 pieces exhibiting less than 25 percent cortex. All 11 striking platforms present in the sample were plain unfaceted surfaces. Five different material types were used including chert (5), silicified limestone (4), andesite (3), quartzite (3), and rhyolite (1). All this material is locally available in the Santa Rita Mountains.

The remaining items were identified as tools, including a scraper, a hammerstone, and two cores. The scraper, made on a quartzite chunk, is unusual because it is roughly rectangular in shape, with two contiguous flat surfaces and two modified edges, with flakes removed using both flat surfaces as platforms. It measures 5.3 cm long by 2.8 cm wide by 2.1 cm thick. The two cores are quite different from each other. One, a silicified limestone cobble fragment, is very small (5.6 cm by 3.9 cm by 4.0 cm), has over 50 percent cortex remaining, and has flakes removed in a multidirectional fashion. The second is a large (11 cm by 5.5 cm by 5.3 cm) piece of quartzite with bidirectional flake removal and no remaining cortex. The hammerstone is an andesite cobble with evidence of battering on all the margins. It is extremely dense, weighing 513 g and measuring 8.2 cm by 7.4 cm by 5.9 cm, making it attractive for hammering tasks.

Ground Stone

One complete handstone, or one-handed mano, was found in Feature 1. It is an irregularly-shaped quartzite cobble (11.2 cm long

Table 4.3

COUNTS AND ATTRIBUTES RECORDED FOR CHIPPED STONE
ARTIFACTS RECOVERED FROM AZ EE:1:91

Recorded Attributes	Debitage	Scrapers	Core	Hammerstone	Total
Artifact type					
Complete flakes	7				7
Proximal flake fragments	4				4
Medial-distal flake fragments	5				5
Size Class					
≤ 2	3				3
≤ 3	5				5
≤ 4	5				5
≤ 5	2				2
> 5	1				1
Percent Cortex					
0-25	13				13
26-75	2				2
76-100	1				1
Material type					
Chert	5				5
Silicified limestone	4		1		5
Andesite	3			1*	4
Quartzite	3	1	1		5
Rhyolite	1				1
Platform type					
Plain	11				11

* With the exception of this hammerstone from Feature 2, all artifacts
were recovered from Feature 1.

by 8.7 cm wide by 4.8 cm thick) with grinding wear on one face, and one edge. The other edges appear to have been slightly ground or smoothed.

Pollen and Flotation Analyses

Two pollen samples were analyzed, one from the floor of Feature 1 and one from the base of the Feature 1 floor pit. Unfortunately neither sample yielded preserved pollen grains.

One flotation sample from the Feature 1 floor pit was analysed. Three pieces of carbonized graythorn (Condalia spathulata) wood were identified, and other wood charcoal was present but unidentifiable. Graythorn does not presently grow in the immediate site area, but is available nearby.

Discussion

Stone terraces, such as those at AZ EE:1:91, are present at sites from southern Arizona through Sonora, Mexico. Although the morphology, abundance, and arrangement of stone features on these sites is extremely variable, two different site types have been distinguished in the Tucson Basin. The first type has been called cerros de trincheras (Stacy 1971), and consists of walls, terraces and other dry-laid masonry features of local, unshaped stone located on volcanic hills. These have been interpreted as defensible, fortified refuges (Wilcox 1979; Fontana and others 1959). Only six of these sites are known in or near the Tucson Basin, all occurring on dark volcanic hills just west of the Santa Cruz River (Fig. 4.5; Fish and others 1982: 55-56). A long, dry-laid wall complex, which could also fall into this category, is known to exist on the east side of the Tortolita Mountains, but it has not been investigated at this time.

The second site type is large agricultural fields containing dry-laid contour terraces, rock piles, check dams, and rock rings of various shapes. Occurring on the bajadas or terraces of major mountain ranges, 18 of these sites are known in the Tucson Basin, with all but two on the fringes of the Tortolita Mountains (Fig. 4.5). All the sites of both types that could be placed temporally appear to date to the early Classic period, with Tanque Verde Red-on-brown representing the dominant ceramic type present.

AZ EE:1:91 does not fall into either of these site classes, for there are neither fortification or defensive features, nor agricultural terraces or related features. Excavations of terraces at Los Morteros did reveal structures in some of the features, defined as residential terraces (Fish and others 1982: 59-61). The features were constructed by clearing a level area on a slope, and partially enclosing the area

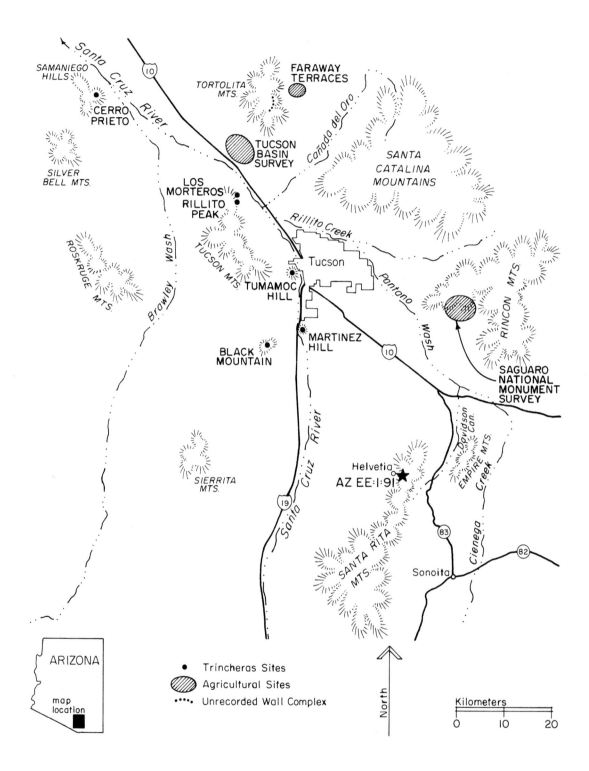

Figure 4.5 Map showing the locations of trincheras and agricultural sites with dry-laid rock walls in and near the Tucson Basin.

with a semicircular or rectangular dry-laid rock wall, leaving the uphill side open. Excavations at two features of this type revealed Tanque Verde phase pit houses 25 cm to 40 cm below ground surface with walls rarely exceeding 50 cm in height. These structures were associated with abundant agricultural terraces (Fish and others 1982: 59-61). Two similar features were also excavated in the New River Valley north of Phoenix, consisting of stacked cobble masonry walls totally encompasing, or in a crescent shape around, the structure (Doyel 1984: 4-5). They were termed field houses, and were situated overlooking agricultural fields or canals.

Although no obvious agricultural field areas are present nearby, the structures at AZ EE:1:91 resemble the houses described above. As noted, at the other sites these structures were considered to be seasonal field houses related to the working of fields. Since this situation does not seem to apply to AZ EE:1:91, it is probable that the structures at this site represent an effort to modify steeply sloping topography to accommodate typical structure types of the Hohokam. This seems even more likely considering the total lack of features such as these at Hohokam sites on the lower, more level ridges in the Rosemont area (Ferg and others 1984). It is possible that this is a special activity site, which might explain why it is located on this moderately steep slope instead of more favorable, flatter areas readily available at lower elevations. Floral and faunal resources may have been available in this area that were not abundant or were lacking in the valleys below. It is also possible that agriculture may have been done somewhere in the area, taking advantage of the steep slopes for runoff irregation, but not as extensive or obvious as those large fields mentioned earlier with various dry-land features. Unfortunately, the artifact assemblage and sample analyses do little to support these ideas and certainly do not aid in determining the types of activities that prompted selection of this locus for settlement.

The sparsity of material culture from AZ EE:1:91 would suggest a short-term or seasonal occupation of the site. The work that would have gone into the building of the house platforms makes it difficult to believe that these were just temporary structures, so it seems more likely that this was a seasonal resource exploitation site, or that it was a site only occupied for a brief period. It is comparable to late Rincon phase sites like AZ EE:2:106 and AZ EE:2:109 in the Rosemont area (Ferg and others 1984), with its small quantity of artifacts and few houses. It also presents the same question of whether all the structures are contemporaneous, or were built in small groups over a period of time.

The few decorated sherds indicate a late Rincon/early Tanque Verde phase occupation of the site (A.D. 1100-1300). This age corresponds well to other sites with dry-laid masonry features that have been dated in the Tucson Basin. This might suggest that dry-laid masonry was an architectural trait newly acquired or popularized in the Tanque Verde phase, since it is rare or lacking in earlier phases but

more common in the later Tucson phase. The temporal placement of the
site would also mean that AZ EE:1:91 was occupied after the abandonment
of the majority of the Hohokam sites in the nearby Rosemont area, which
terminated by the late Rincon phase.

Conclusions

The analysis of features and artifacts from AZ EE:1:91 reveals a
late Rincon/early Tanque Verde phase occupation of the site, but does
little to indicate its functional use. Comparisons with other sites in
the Tucson Basin indicate that dry-laid features such as these are
usually associated with fortified hills or agricultural fields. Since
AZ EE:1:91 does not seem to fit into either of these categories and
since more ideal places for permanent villages are abundant on the lower
ridges, it is felt that these residential terraces represent an
adaptation to the specific topography of the area for use in
specialized activities such as floral or faunal exploitation, or some
type of less obvious agricultural activity utilizing the steep slopes
near the site.

REFERENCES

Agenbroad, Larry D.
    1970   Culture Implications from the Statistical Analysis of a
             Prehistoric Lithic Site in Arizona. MS, master's thesis,
             Department of Anthropology, University of Arizona, Tucson.

Amsden, Charles A.
    1935   The Pinto Basin artifacts. In "The Pinto Basin Site" by
             Elizabeth W. Crozer Campbell and William H. Campbell.
             Southwest Museum Papers 9: 33-51. Los Angeles: Southwest
             Museum.

Carlson, Roy L.
    1965   Eighteenth Century Navajo Fortresses of the Gobernador
             District: The Earl Morris Papers, No. 2. University of
             Colorado Studies, Series in Anthropology 10. Boulder.

Cattanach, George S., Jr.
    1966   A San Pedro Stage Site near Fairbank, Arizona. The Kiva 32:
             1-24.

Deaver, William L.
    1984   Pottery. In "Hohokam Habitation Sites in the Northern Santa
             Rita Mountains," by Alan Ferg, Kenneth C. Rozen, William L.
             Deaver, Martyn D. Tagg, David A. Phillips, Jr., and David A.
             Gregory. Arizona State Museum Archaeological Series 147(2).
             Tucson: University of Arizona.

Di Peso, Charles C.
    1951   The Babocomari Village Site on the Babocomari River,
             southeastern Arizona. The Amerind Foundation 5. Dragoon,
             Arizona: The Amerind Foundation.

    1953   The Sobaipuri Indians of the upper San Pedro Valley,
             southeastern Arizona. The Amerind Foundation 6. Dragoon,
             Arizona: Amerind Foundation.

    1956   The upper Pima of San Cayetano del Tumacacori: An
             archaeohistorical reconstruction of the Ootam of the Pimeria
             Alta. The Amerind Foundation 7. Dragoon, Arizona: The
             Amerind Foundation.

Doyel, David E.
    1977   Excavations in the middle Santa Cruz River Valley,
             southeastern Arizona. Arizona State Museum Contribution to
             Highway Salvage Archaeology in Arizona 44. Tucson:
             University of Arizona.

Doyel, David E.
  1984   Sedentary Period Hohokam Paleo-Economy in the New River
          Drainage, Central Arizona. MS, Arizona State Museum Library,
          University of Arizona, Tucson.

Ferg, Alan
  1981   An Archaeological Survey of a Parcel of Land Added to the
          ANAMAX-Rosemont Land Exchange Area. MS, Arizona State Museum
          Library, University of Arizona, Tucson.

Ferg, Alan, Kenneth C. Rozen, William L. Deaver, Martyn D. Tagg,
David A. Phillips, Jr., and David A. Gregory
  1984   Hohokam habitation sites in the northern Santa Rita
          Mountains. Arizona State Museum Archaeological Series
          147(2). Tucson: University of Arizona.

Fish, Suzanne K., Paul R. Fish and Christian Downum
  1982   Hohokam Terraces and Agricultural Production in the Tucson
          Basin. Paper presented at the Tucson Basin Conference,
          Tucson.

Fontana, Bernard L., J. Cameron Greenleaf, and Donelly Cassidy
  1959   A fortified Arizona mountain. The Kiva 25(2): 41-52.

Gifford, Edward W.
  1932   The southeastern Yavapai. University of California
          Publications in American Archaeology and Ethnology 29(3):
          177-252. Berkeley: University of California.

Greenleaf, J. Cameron
  1975   The Fortified Hill Site near Gila Bend, Arizona. The Kiva
          40(4): 213-282.

Gregory, David A.
  1979   The Tonto-Roosevelt area. In "An Archaeological Survey of
          the Cholla-Saguaro Transmission Line Corridor, Vol. 1,"
          assembled by Lynn S. Teague and Linda L. Mayro. Arizona
          State Museum Archaeological Series 135(1): 175-266. Tucson:
          University of Arizona.

  1981   Western Apache archaeology: Problems and approaches. In
          "The Protohistoric Period in the North American Southwest,
          A.D. 1450-1700," edited by David R. Wilcox and W. Bruce
          Masse. Arizona State University Anthropological Research
          Papers 24.

Hammack, Laurens C.
  1971   The Peppersauce Wash project: A preliminary report on the
          salvage excavation of four archaeological sites in the San
          Pedro Valley, southeastern Arizona. MS, Arizona State Museum
          Library, University of Arizona, Tucson.

Harrington, Mark R.
    1957   A Pinto site at Little Lake, California. Southwest Museum
            Papers 17. Los Angeles: Southwest Museum.

Haury, Emil W.
    1976   The Hohokam: Desert Farmers and Craftsmen. Tucson:
            University of Arizona Press.

Huckell, Bruce B.
    1980   The ANAMAX-Rosemont testing project: Review draft. MS,
            Arizona State Museum Library, University of Arizona, Tucson.

    1981   An archaeological survey of two parcels of land added to the
            ANAMAX-Rosemont land exchange area. MS, Arizona State Museum
            Library, The University of Arizona, Tucson.

    1984   The Archaic occupation of the Rosemont area, northern Santa
            Rita Mountains, southeastern Arizona. Arizona State Museum
            Archaeological Series 147(1). Tucson: University of
            Arizona.

Hungerford, Roger
    1981   Supplemental game species inventory of the Rosemont area. In
            "An Environmental Inventory of the Rosemont Area in Southern
            Arizona, Volume III: The 1981 Supplemental Report." MS,
            Arizona State Museum Library, University of Arizona, Tucson.

Kelly, Isabel T.
    1978   The Hodges Ruin: A Hohokam community in the Tucson Basin.
            Anthropological Papers of the University of Arizona 30.
            Tucson: University of Arizona.

Leach, B.F.
    1969   The Concept of Similarity in Prehistoric Studies. University
            of Otago Anthropology Paper 1.

Lowe, Charles H.
    1981   The vegetation and flora of the Sycamore Canyon area and
            Deering Spring area in the Santa Rita Mountains, Arizona. In
            "An Environmental Inventory of the Rosemont Area in Southern
            Arizona, Volume III: The Supplemental Report." MS, Arizona
            State Museum Library, University of Arizona, Tucson.

Lowe, Charles H., and Cecil R. Schwalbe
    1981   Fishes, amphibians, and reptiles of the Sycamore Canyon area
            and Deering Spring area in the Santa Rita Mountains. In "An
            Environmental Inventory of the Rosemont Area in Southern
            Arizona, Volume III: The 1981 Supplemental Report." MS,
            Arizona State Museum Library, University of Arizona, Tucson.

Nentvig, Juan
    1980   Rudo Ensays: A Description of Sonora and Arizona in 1764.
            Translated by Alberto F. Pradeau and Robert R. Rasmussen.
            Tucson: University of Arizona Press.

Nie, Norman, C. Hadlai Hull, Jean G. Jenkins, Karen Steinbrenner, and Dale Bent
   1975   Statistical Package for the Social Sciences, New York: McGraw-Hill Book Co.

Petryszyn, Yar
   1981   Mammals of the supplemental areas-Rosemont region. In "An Environmental Inventory of the Rosemont Area in Southern Arizona, Volume III: The 1981 Supplemental Report." MS, Arizona State Museum Library, University of Arizona, Tucson.

Pfefferkorn, Ignaz
   1949   Sonora: A Description of the Province. Translated and annotated by Theodore E. Treutlein. Albuquerque: University of New Mexico Press.

Rozen, Kenneth C.
   1979   Lithic analysis and interpretation. In "The AEPCO Project, Volume II, Dos Condado to Apache Survey and Data Recovery of Archaeological Resources," by Deborah Westfall, Kenneth C. Rozen, and Howard M. Davidson. Arizona State Museum Archaeological Series 117: 209-321. Tucson: University of Arizona.

   1981   Patterned associations among lithic techology, site content, and time: Results of the TEP St. Johns Project lithic analysis. In "Prehistory of the St. Johns area, East-Central Arizona: The TEP St. Johns Project," by Deborah Westfall. Arizona State Musuem Archaeological Series 153: 157-232. Tucson: University of Arizona.

   1984   Flaked stone. In "Hohokam Habitation Sites in the Northern Santa Rita Mountains," by Alan Ferg, Kenneth C. Rozen, William L. Deaver, Martyn D. Tagg, David A. Phillips, Jr., and David A. Gregory. Arizona State Museum Archaeological Series 147(2). Tucson: University of Arizona.

Russell, Frank
   1908   The Pima Indians. 26th Annual Report of the Bureau of American Ethnology. Washington: Government Printing Office.

Russell, S. M., and S. Goldwasser
   1981   A supplemental inventory of birds of the Rosemont area. In "An Environmental Inventory of the Rosemont Area in Southern Arizona, Volume III: The 1981 Supplemental Report." MS, Arizona State Musuem Library, University of Arizona, Tucson.

Simmons, Mark, and Frank Turley
   1980   Southwestern Colonial Ironwork: The Spanish Blacksmithing Tradition From Texas to California. Santa Fe: Museum of New Mexico Press.

Simpson, Kay, and Susan J. Wells
    1984   Archeological survey in the eastern Tucson Basin. <u>Western</u> <u>Archeological and Conservation Center Publications in</u> <u>Anthropology</u> 22.

Stacy, V. K. Pheriba
    1974   Cerros De Trincheras in the Arizona Papaguería. MS, doctoral dissertation, Department of Anthropology, University of Arizona, Tucson.

Tagg, Martyn D.
    1983   Archaeological testing at the Abused Ridge Site (AZ BB:9:120), an early Tanque Verde site in the Tucson Basin. MS, Arizona State Museum Library, University of Arizona, Tucson.

    1984   Utilitarian ground stone. In "Hohokam Habitation Sites in the Northern Santa Rita Mountains," by Alan Ferg, Kenneth C. Rozen, William L. Deaver, Martyn D. Tagg, David A. Phillips, Jr., and David A. Gregory. <u>Arizona State Museum</u> <u>Archaeological Series</u> 147(2). Tucson: University of Arizona.

Whalen, Norman M.
    1971   Cochise Culture Sites in the Central San Pedro Drainage, Arizona. MS, doctoral dissertation, Department of Anthropology, University of Arizona, Tucson.

Wilcox, David R.
    1979   Warfare implications of dry-laid masonry walls on Tumamoc Hill. In "The Tumamoc Hill Survey: An Intensive Study of a <u>Cerro de Trincheras</u> in Tucson, Arizona." <u>The Kiva</u> 45(1-2): 15-38.

Windmiller, Ric
    1972   Ta-E-Wun: A Colonial Hohokam campsite. <u>Arizona State Museum</u> <u>Archaeological Series</u> 11. Tucson: University of Arizona.